# 100

## THINGS TO DO IN

# ANNAPOLIS

## AND THE EASTERN SHORE

## BEFORE YOU

# DIE

2nd Edition

# 100

## THINGS TO DO IN
# ANNAPOLIS
## AND THE EASTERN SHORE
## BEFORE YOU
# DIE

• • • • • • • • • • • • • • • • • • • • • • • • • • •

## SUSAN MOYNIHAN

REEDY PRESS

Permissions may be sought directly from Reedy Press at the above mailing address or via our website at reedypress.com.

Library of Congress Control Number: 2024949023

ISBN: 9781681065076

Design by Jill Halpin

Cover photo courtesy of George Sass for Chesapeake Bay Maritime Museum

Unless otherwise noted, all photos are courtesy of the author or believed to be in the public domain.

Printed in the United States of America
25 26 27 28 29    5 4 3 2 1

# DEDICATION

To Mom, for always supporting my
curiosity and love of adventure.

Thomas Point Shoal Lighthouse

# CONTENTS

## Music and Entertainment

• • • • • • • • • • • • • • • • • • • • • • • • • •

• • • • • • • • • • • • • • • • • • • • • •

• • • • • • • • • • • • • • • • • • • • • • • • •

## Shopping and Fashion

• • • • • • • • • • • • • • • • • • • • • •

# ACKNOWLEDGMENTS

A special thanks to everyone who shared their favorite places and experiences, joined me on adventures, and works to protect our history and environment. You are what makes my Annapolis so special.

Ann Moynihan
Barbara, Pat, and Claire Moynihan
Joy and JJ Moynihan
Jeff Nicklason
Daphne Glover Ferrier
Bob Ferrier
Lynne Forsmann
Caroline Foster
Kimberly and Michael Lungociu
Meg Viviano
Jinny Amundson
Erynn Jenkins Powers
Megan Padilla
Christine Ciarmello
Nancy Polstein
Annapolis Green
Save Greenbury Point
Eastport Democratic Club
Maritime Republic of Eastport

• • • • • • • • • • • • • • • • • • • • • • • •

Looking for something else to do? These are my go-to local resources to find out what's happening.

Beepr Buzz
Naptown Scoop
Chesapeake Bay Media
UpStArt Annapolis
Eye on Annapolis
The Baltimore Banner
Historic Homes of Annapolis
Secrets of the Eastern Shore
Visit Annapolis
Visit Maryland
What's Up? Annapolis

# PREFACE

How can you encapsulate Annapolis and Maryland's Eastern Shore in a single book? Annapolis is the country's most charming state capital, founded in the late 1600s and home to a thriving community that continues to grow as it holds fast to its roots. Just across the Bay Bridge, the low-lying Eastern Shore is the realm of watermen who harvest the bounty of the Chesapeake, farmers who keep agriculture the number-one industry in Maryland, and small heritage towns that juggle tradition and transformation. It's impossible to cover everything that makes this region so special, so consider this book an introduction and guide for getting out there and discovering it for yourself.

I grew up in a Navy family, and for much of my childhood we moved from place to place as my father's job dictated. When he left active service and my parents could finally choose a place on their own to call home, they chose Annapolis. I'm so grateful! That decision helped shape who I am. To this day, I never miss a chance to get out on a boat, which I credit to summers sailing on the Severn, and I have a deep love for history, fostered by living in a centuries-old town.

I left home for college and then went further afield to pursue my dreams. But even when I lived elsewhere, Annapolis remained home base. Part of the joy for me of returning was seeing how much Annapolis had stayed the same: our cozy downtown, with its brick-lined streets and independent shops and restaurants; day

• • • • • • • • • • • • • • • • • • • • • • • •

trips or weekends "over the bridge" to explore St. Michaels or Chestertown; steamed crabs every summer on the back porch.

The first edition of this book came out in the fall of 2019—just in time for a worldwide pandemic. I think more has changed here since the pandemic than it did since my high-school days. There's a new influx of wealth, generational changeovers of businesses, and the impact of climate change on rising waters and receding land, from City Dock to low-lying regions of the Eastern Shore. But this region has always been about adapting to change; you have to be when you sit at the crossroads of the Chesapeake Bay and are a founding site in this nation's formation.

As with the first book, I kept my focus on things that reflect, embody, or are created by the people who live here—things that wouldn't be the same (or even exist) anywhere else. And it was all about getting out there and doing. As I traveled around the region doing research, I kept two questions in mind: "Is this worth going over the bridge?" and "Would I bring a friend here?" Everything that made it in the book got double yeses. There are many more things out there to do, I know, but this is a start.

If you're visiting, I hope this inspires you to get out and about—and gives you lots of reasons to come back. If you've recently moved to the area, welcome! I hope this helps you get to know your new home on a deeper level. If you're a longtime local, I hope you discover things that are new to you or get the urge to revisit something and see it in a new way. My aim is to give every reader myriad reasons to get out there and experience this beautiful part of the world

I'm so grateful to make Annapolis my home. And I'm proud to share it with you.

• • • • • • • • • • • • • • • • • • • • • • • •

Oxford-Bellevue Ferry

Crabcakes at Boatyard Bar & Grill

# FOOD
# AND DRINK

# SLAM AN OYSTER SHOOTER
## AT MIDDLETON'S

Former Middleton Tavern owner Jerry Hardesty claimed that he invented the oyster shooter. Which is doubtful—culinary historians point it back to the Gold Rush days—but who cares? It's a great reason to go to this tavern, established in 1750 as an "Inn for Seafaring Men." The recipe is simple: Take a freshly shucked oyster, plop it into a shot glass, and top with a shot of vodka and a dab of house cocktail sauce. Then tip your head back, open the hatch, and down it goes. It's a rite of passage for some locals, and a treat for others. And if you hate it, be happy knowing you never have to do it again.

Middleton Tavern
2 Market Space, Annapolis, 410-263-3323
middletontavern.com

---

### TIP

If you crave something fancier, head across Spa Creek to Boatyard Bar & Grill, where they offer four kinds of shooters, including one with cucumber vodka and cucumber mignonette. Over on Main Street, O'Brien's Oyster Bar and Seafood Tavern offers a half-priced special some weeknights. When in Easton, head to Legal Assets and slurp your shooter under a string of lights on their beautiful patio.

---

## Boatyard Bar & Grill

400 Fourth St., Annapolis, 410-216-6206
boatyardbarandgrill.com

## O'Brien's Oyster Bar & Seafood Tavern

113 Main St., Annapolis, 410-268-6288
obriensoysterbar.com

## Legal Assets

22 S Harrison St., Easton, 443-746-2178
Facebook.com/LegalAssets

# PICK CRABS
## AT A CLASSIC CRAB HOUSE

Picking crabs is a time-honored tradition in these parts. At a true Maryland crab house, the vibe is casual, with indoor/outdoor seating, family-style tables covered in butcher paper, and a dock outside for diners who come by boat. The crabs are doused in Old Bay, then steamed rather than boiled (it keeps the meat moister), and dumped in the center of the table for easy access by everyone. You'll get melted butter for dipping; sides of fresh corn, coleslaw, and rolls; and iced tea or beer to wash it down. Dining is a slow process, especially for newbies as they maneuver the best way to get the meat from the crab's various crevices. But the slow pace is part of the joy, with the focus as much on together time as it is on eating.

# 3 PLACES TO TRY THEM

### Jimmy Cantler's Riverside Inn

Don't let the long lines dissuade you. Wood-paneled Cantler's is the real deal, started in 1974 by a fifth-generation waterman and still family-run.

458 Forest Beach Rd., Annapolis, 410-757-1311
cantlers.com

### Mike's Crab House

This circa-1958 spot on the South River is where Annapolitans go when they want to avoid the crowds at Cantler's.

3030 Riva Rd., Edgewater, 410-956-2784
mikescrabhouse.com

### Fisherman's Crab Deck

Sitting on the waterfront deck, listening to live music, and picking fresh crabs is about as summer as you can get (and it's not open in the winter).

3032 Kent Narrows Way N, Grasonville, 410-827-6666
crabdeck.com

# GET A JOLT
## AT RISE UP COFFEE ROASTERS

Seattle has Starbucks. Boston has Dunkin'. We have Rise Up. Cofounder Tim Cureton discovered the power of great java while bouncing around coffee-growing countries after a stint with the Peace Corps. He founded Rise Up in 2005 as a drive-through coffee stand in St. Michaels. It's since grown into 12 locations in Maryland, plus one in Delaware, and their coffee is sold at grocery stores, including Whole Foods. They make great coffee, following a simple philosophy: Grown by Friends, Roasted by Friends, Enjoyed by Friends.

Fresh organic, free-trade coffee beans are imported and roasted at their facility in Easton. Their six classic styles range from light to dark roast, and they have specials like single-origin Pura Vida, from Costa Rica. I also love the company's distinctive style, heavy on black and white graphics with an indie-inclusive sensibility.

Rise Up HQ
612 Dover Rd., Easton, 410-822-1353
riseupcoffee.com

## TIP

In 2020, Tim and his brother Brett
Cureton paired up to start Rude Food. The
Rude stands for "rudimentary," reflecting
the back-to-basics approach they bring to their
three restaurants, Rude Burger, Rude BBQ,
and La Bodega—all delicious and all in
Easton. Don't miss the bourbon slushies.

# COUNT THE LAYERS
## OF A SMITH ISLAND CAKE

There are multiple theories as to the origins of Maryland's state dessert. One says that generations ago, Smith Island women would try to outdo each other at community cake walks by presenting cakes with the most amount of layers. Another says women would bake one layer for each hour their waterman husbands were out at sea; the more layers, the harder working the husband. The traditional cake is 8 to 10 layers of yellow cake with a chocolate fudge frosting that stands up to the elements, but you'll also find flavors such as lemon cream, coconut, and red velvet.

Smith Island Bakery, located on island in Ewell, sells fresh cakes or slices to visitors who come out by boat. Smith Island Baking Co. is a larger family-owned bakery on the mainland in Crisfield that ships to restaurants and homes around the country.

Smith Island Bakery
20926 Caleb Jones Rd., Ewell, 410-425-2018
smithislandbakeryllc.com

Smith Island Baking Company
45 W Chesapeake Ave., Crisfield, 410-425-CAKE
smithislandcake.com

# HAVE A REUNION
## AT MCGARVEY'S

If there's one bar that's synonymous with Annapolis and the Naval Academy, it would be McGarvey's. Evidence: When the Academy hired USNA alumna Vice Admiral Yvette Davids as commandant, members of her class of 1990 took over the back room for a happy-hour reunion celebrating her. It's that kind of place. But it's not just the Academy. The bar staff is so loved by locals that longtime bartender Martin "Beans" Gardner was named grand marshal of the 2024 Annapolis St. Patrick's Day Parade. It's that kind of place too.

The front room is especially lovely in late afternoon when the wooden bar gleams with filtered sunlight and the evening crowds haven't yet descended. Pair a dozen freshly shucked oysters with a pint of Aviator lager and raise a toast of thanks to the pilots who served our country and who are represented by the flight helmets proudly displayed above the bar.

8 Market Space, Annapolis
410-263-5700
mcgarveysannapolis.com

# DISCOVER THE MAGIC
## OF A MARYLAND CRAB CAKE

If there is one dish that defines us, it would be the crab cake, found on menus from dive bars to five-star restaurants. We Marylanders are deeply picky about our cakes. I've traveled the world, but I rarely eat them outside of Maryland, because they never measure up. We all have our favorite recipe, often passed down through the family. But the common denominator is local blue crab (jumbo lump, please), a moistener (usually egg or mayo), and a hint of binding agent or seasoning: just enough to hold the meat together when the cakes go under the broiler or into the frying pan.

Also, make sure you seek out Maryland crabmeat. The Chesapeake Bay's brackish water and cold winters make our crabs sweeter and fatter than you'll find in warmer-weather crabbing spots like the Gulf of Mexico or Venezuela. It may cost more, but you'll be rewarded with a richer, sweeter crabcake—and the knowledge that you're supporting longstanding Chesapeake maritime culture.

# BEST PLACES TO TRY THEM

### Boatyard Bar & Grill

The perfect, softball-sized cakes at this lively Eastport sailor's bar bear the slogan "all killer, no filler" and count the late Jimmy Buffett and me as fans.

400 Fourth St., Annapolis, 410-216-6206
boatyardbarandgrill.com

### Edgewater Restaurant

This unpretentious family-run eatery hasn't changed much since 1948, and neither has their crab-cake recipe. Their meaty all-lump cakes draw fans from all over Delmarva.

148 Mayo Rd., Edgewater
410-956-3202

### Dock Street Bar & Grill

This City Dock staple pairs their meaty jumbo lump cakes with a craveworthy whole-grain mustard tartar sauce.

136 Dock St., Annapolis, 410-268-7278
dockstreetbar.com

# GET A TASTE OF JAMES BEARD
## AT BAS ROUGE

James Beard is to chefs what Oscar is to film directors. In 2024, the Eastern Shore got its first James Beard Award, when Executive Chef Harley Peet of Bas Rouge was named Best Chef: Mid-Atlantic. Inspired by classic European fine dining tradition, Bas Rouge excels in the details, with creative dishes as beautiful as they are delicious. The menu changes frequently, based on seasonality, and incorporates the best ingredients from around the world paired with the best locally sourced, including greens from Peet's own garden. The wine list spans 2,500 bottles, and the decor is elegant enough to match the cuisine without feeling stuffy.

19 Federal St., Easton
410-822-1637
basrougeeaston.com

---

### TIP

Bluepoint Hospitality owns multiple restaurants in downtown Easton, all under the purview of Chef Peet and all delicious in their own way. Other standouts include housemade ice cream at Bonheur, crepes at P. Bordier and wood-fired pizza at Roma.

bluepointhospitality.com

---

# INDULGE IN HOMESTYLE COOKING
## AT OLD SALTY'S

It isn't easy to get to Old Salty's, but that's part of the appeal. Driving the back roads of Dorchester County, through lowland marsh and tidal flats, forces you to slow down and appreciate where you are. Which is a great mindset to have when you get there.

Set in the town's former schoolhouse, this restaurant opened in the 1980s with the aim of featuring family recipes and local ingredients, long before that was a thing. Everything starts with yeast rolls and butter. For crab cakes, take your pick of back fin or jumbo lump, served broiled or fried. The imperial is the best I've ever had, creamy yet zesty, complementing the crab without overpowering it. Take advantage of seasonal specials and sides, often based on what's available in nearby gardens. And don't even get me started about their pies. Those alone are worth the drive. Summer weekends bring live music to their outdoor tiki bar.

2560 Hoopers Island Rd., Fishing Creek, 410-397-3752
oldsaltys.com

# SAY THE PLEDGE OF ALLEGIANCE
## AT CHICK & RUTH'S

When Chick and Ruth Levitt opened their sandwich shop in 1965, they had no idea it would grow into a beloved Annapolis institution. The Levitts retired in 2017 and sold the deli to loyal customer Keith Jones, who vowed to keep it the same way. When Keith's son Spencer took over in 2021, he vowed the same. You'll still find the bright yellow-and-orange color scheme, vintage chrome counter, and walls crammed with signed celebrity photos. Each day starts with the Pledge of Allegiance, done at 8:30 a.m. on weekdays and 9:30 a.m. on weekends. Breakfast is served all day, and the menu includes a slew of sandwiches named after politicians. Bring your appetite to attempt their Colossal Challenge (featured on *Man vs. Food*). Finish in time and the meal is on them, with a T-shirt as proof.

165 Main St., Annapolis, 410-269-6737
chickandruths.com

# EAT LIKE A CAVEMAN
## AT MODERN STONE AGE KITCHEN

A lot of places say they make things from scratch, but Modern Stone Age Kitchen takes it to a whole new level. It's an outgrowth of the Eastern Shore Food Lab, created in 2017 as a research lab to study how ancestral foodways can optimize nutrition today. Dr. Bill Schindler and his wife, Christina, have turned the ethos into a unique, delicious restaurant where everything is made in-house, using natural ingredients like unrefined maple syrup paired with healthy techniques including in-house fermentation and a nose-to-tail approach to butchery.

The dishes speak for themselves. I'm all about the house-roasted chicken salad with scratch aioli, and on Fridays they do wood-fired pizza, with everything house-made from dough to cheese to pepperoni. The onsite bakery sells sourdough breads, bagels, and cookies to go.

236 Cannon St., Chestertown, 410-996-4776
modernstoneagekitchen.com

# FIND SOMETHING FOR EVERYONE
## AT BREAD AND BUTTER KITCHEN

If kitchens are the hub of a home, consider this Kitchen a hub of the Annapolis community. Owner Monica Alvarado spent 20 years in tech when, approaching burnout, she started a food blog and got to know area farmers and producers. That led to her opening her own restaurant, open for breakfast and lunch only, with seasonal, scratch-made meals. The menu focuses on local providers, with area farms and makers prominently noted, and has something for every taste and dietary restriction, from meatatarian to vegan and gluten-free.

I love bringing out-of-town friends here. The food is great, there's always a welcoming vibe, and sitting outside at a café table by a thriving marina encapsulates what makes Eastport so special. As is the adjacent coworking/dining/meeting space; called The Hub, it's designed as a gathering place and reflects the good work Monica does in the community.

303 Second St. A, Annapolis, 410-202-8680
breadandbutterkitchen.com

# JOIN CENTURIES OF SOCIALIZERS
## AT REYNOLD'S TAVERN

Hatmaker William Reynolds constructed this brick tavern in 1747. The prime placement of The Beaver and Lac'd Hat (as it was originally known) on Church Circle made it a favorite meeting spot in the Colonial era, and it's just as loved today.

Book afternoon tea in the Victorian-style dining room marked with original wooden floors, antiques, and displays of vintage china, and you'll be presented with a selection of loose teas, along with the tea-time classics: fresh-baked scones, finger sandwiches, and an array of petit sweets to finish. The Beer Garden is a lovely brick-paved back patio with café tables, strings of lights, and events from live music to trivia nights. But for the most historic vibe, head downstairs to the 1747 Pub, which was the original kitchen of Mr. Reynolds's tavern, and still oozes atmosphere with its low ceiling, brick floors, and stone fireplace.

7 Church Cir., Annapolis, 410-295-9555
reynoldstavern.org

# BET ON THE BOOZE TRIFECTA
## IN ST. MICHAELS

Cheers to four boozy options within a single city block in the Old Mill District. Start off at Windon Distilling Company's micro distillery, which offers tastes of their stellar Lyon Rum and whiskeys, along with samples from Gray Wolf Craft Distilling, known for Maryland-style rye and sassafras-rested gin. Next, head to St. Michaels Winery, which offers inexpensive samples of 18 varietals. End your tour at Eastern Shore Brewery; the oldest microbrewery on the Eastern Shore, they've won state awards for their Back Creek Blonde. The brewery is part tasting room (they have 10 on tap, plus cans and growlers to go) and part neighborhood hangout, with darts, tabletop shuffleboard, and live music.

Lyon Rum/Windon Distilling
605 S Talbot St., 443-333-9181
lyonrum.com

St. Michaels Winery
609 S Talbot St., 410-745-0808
stmichaelswinery.com

Gray Wolf Craft Distilling
605 S Talbot St., 443-339-4894
graywolfspirits.com

Eastern Shore Brewing
605 S Talbot St., 410-714-1999
easternshorebrewing.com

# BUY FROM A WATERMAN
## AT WILD COUNTRY SEAFOOD

For most of its existence, Eastport was home to hundreds of watermen who fished the Bay and sold their catch at the dock each morning. Those days are gone, but Pat Mahoney is working hard to keep the tradition alive. He learned how to work the Bay from his father, Pat Senior, and by the age of 14 was out trot-lining for crabs in his own skiff. They opened Wild Country with a simple premise: Catch fresh seafood, then sell it—ideally on the same day. Their boats, *Baby Boy* and *Wild Country*, are the last commercial workboats in Eastport.

In season, expect fresh crabs and fresh fish, usually rockfish. The oysters, called Patty's Fatty's, come from their aquaculture farm on the Rhode River. I'm partial to their fried oyster platter, served with fries and slaw. It's a simple place, the kind you don't find anymore. Except in Eastport, right where it should be.

124 Bay Shore Ave., Annapolis, 410-267-6711
wildcountryseafood.com

# JOIN THE PARTY
## AT DINNER UNDER THE STARS

Every Wednesday and Saturday night from late May through September, the first block of West Street between Church Circle and Calvert Street is transformed into a European-style outdoor café. The block is closed to vehicle traffic, and the restaurants bring tables out onto the brick-paved street, inviting diners to grab a table and become part of the scene. Strings of lights frame the view of St. Anne's Church, and an ever-changing array of live bands gets people dancing in the street. There are even pickleball courts so you can work up an appetite. Some restaurants take reservations; others don't. If there's a wait, no problem—you can pass the time with some great people-watching.

West St. and Calvert St., Annapolis, 410-858-5884
dinnerunderthestars.org

# SIP AN UPDATED CLASSIC
## AT PARLEY ROOM

Opened in 2023 in an historic hotel across from the State House, this speakeasy-style bar takes inspiration from the 1920s but is thoroughly modern. The cocktail menu notes the creation date of classic cocktails, which the mixologists update with unique tweaks and fresh ingredients in the form of housemade syrups and small-batch liquors. Their old fashioned builds on the original created in 1880, with fig syrup and black walnut bitters. Angels and Demons is a margarita (created in 1938) incorporating St. Germain, cilantro and habanero. The Café Parley transforms an espresso martini (born 1990) with hazelnut and a torched marshmallow. Their small plates are equally fab, be it a custom charcuterie board or torched filet mignon. In cooler months, cozy up in the dimly lit bar. In warmer months the front patio overflows with cocktail aficionados, especially if a DJ is playing.

25 State Circle, 443-837-6481
parleyroom.com

# DINE WITH A HEROINE
## AT KITTY KNIGHT INN

As the story goes, in May 1813, British troops came up the Sassafras River, setting towns on fire along the way. When they attacked Georgetown, resident Kitty Knight confronted them, stomping out flames and demanding they stop, thus sparing her home and that of an elderly neighbor. The surviving buildings, now combined into one, make up the Kitty Knight Inn, a restaurant and inn catering to day trippers and boaters.

In 2022, new owners Jamestown Hotel Group created buzz with the opening of Deep Blue restaurant, which serves Southern-inflected dishes like Old Bay-seared rockfish. The wide patio and dining room have stellar river views, but I also love the tavern out back. Set in the oldest part of the house, it has the original beamed ceiling, two-sided brick fireplace, and a painting of a nude woman that some say might be Kitty herself. Did the British soldiers spare the house because they were fond of the brothel upstairs, as rumor goes? We'll never know, but both stories are great.

14028 Augustine Hermann Hwy., Galena, 410-648-5200
deepbluerestaurant.com

---

### TIP

Check in and make a weekend of it. Kitty Knight Inn has 11 guest rooms, one of them set in Kitty's former bedroom.

---

# MAKE A NEW (OLD) FRIEND
## AT DAVIS' PUB

Every port needs a great sailor's bar, and in Annapolis that's Davis' Pub. Located on Back Creek in Eastport, it started as a 1920s general store, then was a lounge serving local watermen who lived and worked here, before morphing in 1986 into the unpretentious local hangout it is today. Inside is a long bar and a no-frills dining room with a handful of tables, serving up tasty cheesy crab-topped pretzels, Baltimore-style steamed shrimp, and pulled pork sandwiches. I like to bring my dog and sit outside at one of the picnic tables, where you'll invariably overhear someone talking about their recent boat journey. A sign in the window reads, "Where there are no strangers . . . only friends you haven't met." After a few visits, you'll find that to be true.

400 Chester Ave., Annapolis, 410-268-7432
davispub.com

# SAMPLE THE SPECIALS
## AT SAILOR OYSTER BAR

When Sailor Oyster Bar opened in 2016, it quickly became one of the hottest restaurants in Annapolis—until June 2022, when a major fire tore through the circa-1896 building. It remained closed for nearly two years before reopening in 2024 to the joy of every food lover in town.

This eclectic restaurant doesn't have a traditional kitchen; everything is done torched, sous vide or served raw. You'll always find at least six kinds of oysters, some local and some from farther afield, and a selection of imported tinned fish, served with artisanal bread, salted butter, and greens. The daily specials are always inventive, often featuring a fresh take on ceviche or toast, and the cocktails are equally crafty. The retro decor and sailor pinup art is a nod to oyster bars of yore, in a modern, cheeky way.

196 West St., Annapolis, 410-571-5449
sailoroysterbar.com

---

### TIP
The restaurant is small and fills up fast, especially on weekends. No table, no problem; get on the waiting list and head down the street to Metropolitan, where you'll get discounted drinks while you wait.

# PICK WITH THE CROWD
## AT THE ROTARY CRAB FEAST

By sheer numbers, one of the area's biggest parties has to be the Rotary Crab Feast, a charity fundraiser held every August at Navy–Marine Corps Memorial Stadium in Annapolis. Each year, up to 2,500 people gather at 5 p.m. to settle in at long, paper-covered tables for three hours of all-you-can-eat steamed crabs, vats of crab soup, local sweet corn on the cob, plus barbecue, hot dogs, and homemade sweets, all washed down with soda and beer. It's billed as the largest crab feast in the world, and who am I to argue? The event has been going since 1946 and didn't take a break during the pandemic, when feasters picked up crabs to go instead of dining en masse. As usual, all proceeds go to local charities.

annapolisrotary.org/crabfeast

---

### TIP

Looking for another way to feast? The Crab Place in Crisfield offers an annual crab-and-cruise weekend in July, while Choptank Riverboat Company in Hurlock sets sail with Crab Feast cruises on select days from June through September.

crabandcruise.com
suicide-bridge-restaurant.com

---

# CELEBRATE A SPECIAL OCCASION
## AT LEWNES' STEAK HOUSE

Nothing fits a special occasion like a classic steakhouse, and Lewnes' has been the locals' go-to spot for decades. It's as much about the mood as it is about the food, with dry-aged USDA Prime beef (I like the ribeye) and seafood; attentive service that makes you feel looked after but not rushed; and bartenders who know how to make a killer cocktail. The ambiance is elegant yet cozy, with high-backed leather booths, wood-paneled walls, and black-and-white photos. It's almost guaranteed that someone at a nearby table will be celebrating a birthday or anniversary, and I've witnessed engagements there as well. (She said yes.) The restaurant is run by Mack and Sam Lewnes, grandsons of Greek immigrant Sam Lewnes, who opened a corner store on this same spot back in 1921.

401 Fourth St., Annapolis, 410-263-1617
lewnessteakhouse.com

# HIT THE DOCK BARS
## AT KENT NARROWS

Kent Island lies between mainland Maryland and the Eastern Shore—which means umpteen Marylanders go through it at some point on their way to the beach. But you're missing out if you don't pull over, especially on summer weekends, when the dock bars are in full force. The Big Owl Tiki Bar is closest to the channel, with prime views of the Route 50 bridge. Walking down the wooden pier feels like walking into vacation mode, amplified when you grab a dockside stool and order up a crush. Then stroll to the Jetty for crab-topped pizza and live music from top bands around the Mid-Atlantic. My favorite time to kick back is on Sunday afternoons, when the pleasure boats are out in full and the backed-up traffic on the bridge makes you grateful you have no other place to be.

The Big Owl Tiki Bar
3015 Kent Narrow Way S, Grasonville, 410-827-6523
thebigowl.com

The Jetty
201 Wells Cove, Grasonville, 410-827-4959
jettydockbar.com

# STUFF YOUR FACE
## AT A SEAFOOD FESTIVAL

Oyster season officially kicks off in October, overlapping with blue crab season (which runs from April through December). Add in the onset of cooler weather and you have the perfect recipe for a seafood festival! Chesapeake Bay Maritime Museum's OysterFest is a full-day affair with freshly shucked oysters galore, an oyster stew competition, and an oyster slurp-off. Over in Rock Hall, Fall Fest is a street fair with live music and shuckers doing their thing to order.

But it's not just oysters. The two-day Maryland Seafood Festival, held every fall at Sandy Point State Park, has a beer and oyster tent, but also a crab soup cookoff and a crab-cake eating contest. If you can't make the fall events, keep an eye out for Snow Hill's annual oyster roast, an all-you-can-eat festival held at the end of the season in March.

OysterFest, St. Michaels
cbmm.org/event/oysterfest

Rock Hall Fall Fest, Rock Hall
rockhallfallfest.com

Maryland Seafood Festival, Annapolis
abcevents.com/maryland-seafood-festival

Snow Hill Oyster Roast, Snow Hill
snowhillchamber.com/annual-oyster-roast

## TIP

If seafood isn't your thing, keep an eye out for the Maryland Chicken Wing Festival, held every spring at Anne Arundel County Fairgrounds, with live music, a chicken-wing eating competition, and more than 70 flavors of wings for sampling.

Rams Head Tavern

# MUSIC
# AND ENTERTAINMENT

# BE MOVED BY MUSIC
## WITH ANNAPOLIS OPERA COMPANY

The Annapolis Opera Company has been a beloved part of the city's cultural scene than 50 years, and in 1979 became the first resident company at Maryland Hall. They put on three full-scale productions each year (typically October, January and March), spanning classics such as *La Traviata* and *The Barber of Seville* to modern works like Leonard Bernstein's *Trouble in Tahiti*.

In their Opera Insight series, you can join them before the show for pre-performance discussion, where an invited speaker gives greater context on the composer and the meaning and context behind the story. Each run ends with a Sunday matinee, followed by a casual post-performance talk back with the Artistic Director and cast members.

Another favorite event is the Annual Vocal Competition, established in 1988 as a way for young performers to get more involved in the world of opera. It's a great complement to their children's programming, including education and concerts aimed at getting the next generation excited about opera.

801 Chase St., 410-267-8135
annapolisopera.org

# SET THE STAGE
## WITH THE COLONIAL PLAYERS

Founded in 1949, The Colonial Players is the oldest running community theater in Annapolis. But don't let the name fool you; it comes from their setting in Colonial Annapolis, not the slant of their play selection. The 180-seat theater puts on seven shows per season: one musical, one holiday, and five plays. The schedule can include anything from a classic by Neil Simon to lesser-known works like 2024's *Working*, a Steven Schwartz musical based on the groundbreaking book by Studs Terkel. All shows are presented in the round, which leads to creative staging and an up-close experience for attendees. The theater may be small, but it has a big regional presence, consistently winning awards from the Washington Area Community Theater Honors.

108 East St., Annapolis, 410-268-7373
thecolonialplayers.org

---

### TIP

You can purchase tickets per show or subscribe annually with seats to each play. But my favorite way to go is with the FlexTicket, which gets you 10 discounted seats per year, to spread out however you wish throughout the season.

# DANCE ON THE LAWN
## AT TIDES & TUNES

One of the best ways to spend a summer Thursday is at the Annapolis Maritime Museum's annual music series, Tides & Tunes. From mid-June through mid-August, local bands take over an outdoor stage at the museum, overlooking Back Creek. A festive crowd fills the surrounding grassy space with blankets, lawn chairs, kids, and dogs, and the overflow spills out onto the nearby docks, creating an only-in-Annapolis evening. Add in a cash bar and snacks from food trucks and you have all the makings of a perfect summer evening. Concerts showcase everything from folk to rock to reggae, with the biggest turnout going for local fave Dublin 5, whose Irish-tinged rock gets everybody moving. Admission is always free, but donations are gladly accepted. Proceeds from donations and bar sales all benefit the museum.

723 Second St., Annapolis, 410-295-0104
amaritime.org

## TIP
Get there early and tour the museum. Set in a former oyster-packing plant, it celebrates the Bay's heritage via exhibits, lectures, and school programs, giving it an impact much larger than its physical footprint.

# TUNE IN
## AT RAMS HEAD ON STAGE

One of the best things about living in Annapolis is easy access to Rams Head On Stage, the crown jewel of the music scene. What started in 1989 as a basement pub has grown into one of the East Coast's premier music venues, showcasing nationally renowned performers almost every night of the year. The calendar is eclectic and well-curated. You might see a cool indie band one night, a legendary singer–songwriter the next. The cabaret-style theater seats 312, giving each show a uniquely intimate vibe. Wait staff serves light fare and drinks during the show, or you can do a pre- or post-show dinner in the warren of brick-walled dining rooms that make up Rams Head Tavern, their attached restaurant. There's also local live music every weekend in the Rams Head Tavern bar.

33 West St., Annapolis, 410-268-4545
ramsheadonstage.com

## TIP

That original basement pub is still open, tucked under the larger tavern. With its centuries-old brick walls, tiny tables, and low-beamed ceiling, it's a cozy spot for a nightcap, whether you saw a show upstairs or not.

# HAVE A MIGHTY *CRAIC*
## AT GALWAY BAR

*Craic* is the Irish term for a good time, filled with music and fun. And that's what always ends up happening at Galway Bay, a quintessential Irish pub in Annapolis. The vibe is intentionally convivial, with no TVs to distract from the art of conversation. Bartenders greet you like a regular, and an evening there typically involves old and new friends making spirited banter on anything from local news to their Irish ancestry. Wednesday nights bring a traditional Irish jam session, with regulars on button accordion, banjo, and fiddle, and other players dropping in to join. On Sunday afternoons, a singer on acoustic guitar eases you through the waning weekend hours. The restaurant is one of the best in town, with shepherd's pie, lamb stew, and an all-day Irish breakfast, while the bar offers Guinness on draft (along with local craft brews) and the largest selection of whiskeys in Maryland.

63 Maryland Ave., Annapolis, 410-263-8333
galwaybaymd.com

---

### TIP

Galway Bay has three sister spots: Brian Boru in Severna Park, Killarney House in Davidsonville, and Pirate's Cove in Galesville. You'll find the same great food and music at each.

---

# EMBRACE A CENTURY OF THE ARTS
## AT AVALON THEATER

This gem of a theater in Easton originally opened in 1922, wowing vaudeville audiences with its leaded glass doors, 18-foot dome, and electric-pneumatic pipe organ. In the 1930s, it morphed into a movie theater, premiering films by Gary Cooper and Bette Davis. But times changed, and in the 1980s it closed for several years. The city of Easton bought it at auction in 1989, and today the Avalon Foundation runs it as a nonprofit theater. A loving renovation restored its beauty, adding a state-of-the-art sound system. The main theater seats 400 in an Art Deco backdrop of hand-painted gilt-and-red accents and stained-glass skylights under the still-intact dome. Or cozy up in the 60-seat Stoltz Listening Room, a black-box, cabaret-style theater. Whatever your style, the Avalon likely has it. They host national touring acts playing anything from jazz to bluegrass, plus regional bands and singer–songwriters, author readings, stand-up comedy shows, and live opera broadcasts from the Met.

40 E Dover St., Easton, 410-822-7299
avalonfoundation.org

# HUM ALONG
## WITH THE USNA GLEE CLUB

The US Naval Academy's mission is to train the next generation of naval officers, but they also have an incredible music department. The Men's and Women's Glee Clubs are the headline attractions. Their annual performance of Handel's *Messiah* at the USNA Chapel, in conjunction with Annapolis Symphony and Annapolis Opera, is always a sellout and broadcast nationally on PBS. You can also catch them live every fall during Parents' Weekend, and every March at Maryland Hall for their Spring Oratorio, backed by the Annapolis Symphony Orchestra. For something lighter, book tickets for their annual musical, always a full-on Broadway-style production backed by a live pit orchestra.

If you can see only one event, make it the Halloween Concert, a two-night, over-the-top spectacle of laser-light show, dramatic costumes, and organ-backed music performed for a sellout crowd every October at the USNA Chapel.

410-293-2439
Usna.edu/Music

# ATTEND A MUSICAL
## AT SUMMER GARDEN THEATER

Theater under the stars is a summertime tradition in Annapolis, thanks to Summer Garden Theater. Set in a restored 19th-century, brick-and-frame warehouse across from City Dock, this is community theater at its best, run on the power of volunteers, from the actors and crew to the ushers and office staff. The company was founded in 1966, and generations of Annapolitans have grown up enjoying these shows, which run every weekend from Memorial Day to Labor Day. The program focuses on feel-good musicals, blending new works with crowd pleasers, like the 2024 sellout of *Escape to Margaritaville*. The theater is open-air, and the show goes on whatever the weather, be it rain or steamy August heat; that's part of the experience.

143 Compromise St., Annapolis, 410-268-9212
summergarden.com

# SUPPORT A MUSICIAN
## WITH AMFM

A musician's life often comes without a safety net. If you get sick, you can't perform—and there goes your income. Enter the Annapolis Musicians Fund for Musicians. This nonprofit was created in 2006 to offer temporary financial assistance to local professional musicians who cannot work due to sickness, injury or circumstance. Among other programs, they also fund music lessons for students at Bates Middle School, and award a college scholarship to a first-year student majoring in music performance at a four-year institution.

To raise funds, they offer a series of concerts throughout the year called In the Vane Of. Typically held at Rams Head On Stage, each night is dedicated to a certain artist or period of music; a slate of musicians perform a cover from that artist as well as an original inspired by the artist. Past shows have paid tribute to artists from Tom Petty to Prince. It's a great night of music, held several times throughout the year. And keep an eye out for An Annapolis Christmas, which is two nights of holiday-themed tunes. December 2024 marked the 26th year for the festive event.

am-fm.com

## TIP

Another great way to support local musicians is by attending Eastport a Rockin'. This annual day-long party features 35+ local bands, playing on four stages near the Annapolis Maritime Museum. A portion of proceeds go to local causes, including AMFM.

eastportarockin.com

# GET INSPIRED
## AT MARYLAND HALL

It's hard to wrap your head around everything that goes on at this former high school–turned–cultural center in Anne Arundel County. It's home to the Annapolis Symphony Orchestra, Annapolis Opera, Live Arts Maryland, and the Ballet Theatre of Maryland, all of whom perform there throughout the year.

The redone former auditorium brings in big-name concerts and theater. Created from the former gymnasium, the smaller Bowen Theater is a black-box theater easily transformed for plays, film screenings, and improv. Four gallery spaces offer rotating exhibits of painting, photography, sculpture, and experiential installations. The Artist in Residence program allows artists to work in onsite studios and share their process with drop-in guests during the week. And a full slate of classes for kids and adults offers everything from ceramics to digital editing and podcasting in a state-of-the-art recording studio.

801 Chase St., Annapolis, 410-263-5544
marylandhall.org

# DISCOVER THE BACK ROOM
## AT 49 WEST

As the name promises, there's so much more to 49 West Coffeehouse, Winebar & Gallery than coffee. By day, it has a classic coffeehouse vibe, with people reading, working on laptops, and quietly chatting over salads and sandwiches. The restaurant walls double as a gallery for an ever-changing array of local artists, with most of the works for sale.

But many nights, it changes into a music venue, mostly centered on their tiny back room. You never know what you're going to find—acoustic jazz one night, a touring bluegrass band the next. Wednesdays bring a packed house for Hippie Happy Hour, and the monthly songwriter's circle invites local singer–songwriters to share songs and the inspiration behind them. It's always a treat to see performers in such an intimate environment.

49 West St., Annapolis, 410-626-9796
49westcoffeehouse.com

# SCARE YOURSELF SILLY
## ON A GHOST TOUR

Ghost tours are a fantastic way to learn about a town's history, via tales of locals who lived and died there. (OK, so most of them died terribly, but still . . .)

Founded by Michael Carter, author of *Haunted Annapolis*, Annapolis Tours and Crawls leads year-round walking tours that take you down cobblestone streets, into haunted cemeteries and past grand mansions hiding ghastly secrets. Their Haunted Pub Crawl is a fun twist, taking you into historic taverns for drinks and stories.

On the Eastern Shore, no one knows hauntings like Mindie Burgoyne. Her company, Chesapeake Ghost Tours, offers deeply researched ghost walks in nine towns across the Delmarva Peninsula. If you can pick only one, make it Cambridge. Home to lingering spirits of soldiers, jilted women, and a one-legged sea captain, Burgoyne claims High Street is the most haunted street on the Eastern Shore—and she would know.

Annapolis Tours and Crawls
443-534-0043
toursandcrawls.com

Chesapeake Ghost Walks
443-735-0771
chesapeakeghosts.com

### TIP

If ghost walks aren't your thing, but pub crawls are, sign up for Twisted History, where Tours and Crawls co-owner Melissa Huston puts an intriguing, amusing spin on what you think you know about Annapolis.

# GET CLASSICAL
## AT ST. ANNE'S

Set on the second highest point of land in downtown Annapolis, St. Anne's is the city's oldest parish, dating back to the late 1600s. The circa-1859 Romanesque-style church is actually the third St. Anne's building; the first two were lost to expansion and fire, respectively. Inside are unique features such as a brass lectern from the Confederate ship C.S.S. *Shenandoah*; a stunning Tiffany-stained glass window; and charming handmade needlepoint kneelers in the pews, each one unique and made by a parishioner. Equally impressive is the German organ, installed in 1975.

Take it all in during the Bach+ series, done in conjunction with Live Arts Maryland, or the annual performances of Handel's *Messiah*, featuring world-class soloists, Annapolis Chorale, and Annapolis Chamber Orchestra.

Church Cir., Annapolis, 410-276-9333
stannes-annapolis.com

# TOUR A GUITAR FACTORY
## AT PAUL REED SMITH

When a teenaged Paul Smith began building instruments from scratch back in the mid-1970s, no one imagined what his passion would lead to. But today, the Kent Island–based Paul Reed Smith Guitars is one of the premier guitar companies in the world, with a waiting list of up to six months for custom instruments. The free factory tour, held twice weekly, takes you out onto the factory floor to witness the process from start to finish: choosing the wood, cutting and pressing the tops and bottoms, designing the head stocks and mother-of-pearl inlays, and hand-staining each piece in layers to create a beautiful hue and shine. Even if you're not a guitar player or enthusiast (though most people who take it are both), the tour is fascinating.

380 Log Canoe Cir., Stevensville, 410-643-9970
prsguitars.com

# SPEND THE WEEKEND
## AT A MUSIC FESTIVAL

The Let's Go Music Festival kicked off in 2021, and takes over Anne Arundel Fairgrounds every spring for a three-day celebration. The first night is all local, and Saturday and Sunday bring national touring acts from around the country; past acts have included Gin Blossoms, Goo Goo Dolls, and Dashboard Confessional.

In 2022, Rams Head Group launched the Annapolis Songwriters Festival. The four-day festival gathers a who's who of songwriters to play in venues including Rams Head, Maryland Hall, and a large outdoor stage at City Dock, and offer free showcases at bars and restaurants around town. The inaugural 2022 fest had Lucinda Williams and Jake Owens; 2023 had Blondie and Marty Stuart; and 2024 featured Lee Brice and Citizen Cope.

The Annapolis Baygrass Music Festival launched at Sandy Point in 2023. This three-day fest brings in top names in bluegrass and jamgrass, and puts proceeds towards environmental causes and mental health awareness; hence their tagline, "Every Jam Saves the Bay."

letsgofest.com

annapolissongwritersfestival.com

baygrassfestival.com

# TIP

All three festivals offer daily or multi-day admission, and VIP packages that include perks like special seating areas, upgraded food and bar, and more. Act early; the VIPs sell out fast—sometimes before the artist lineup is even announced.

# ENJOY THE MASTERS
## WITH THE ANNAPOLIS SYMPHONY

The Annapolis Symphony Orchestra started organically in 1962, when two local musicians with a shared love of classical music began practicing together during their lunch hours, just for the love of playing. Word soon got out, the group expanded, and now ASO is the largest performing arts group in Anne Arundel County. An ensemble of 70 professional union musicians, led by conductor José-Luis Novo, perform multiple concerts throughout the year, often joined by internationally acclaimed guests. Most concerts are held at Maryland Hall for the Creative Arts, and the ever-changing program ranges from Great Composers and collaborations with the USNA Glee Club to live performances playing along with silent films. Cap off the summer with their annual Pops in the Park concerts, held Labor Day weekend at outdoor amphitheaters at Quiet Waters Park in Annapolis and Downs Park in Pasadena.

801 Chase St., Suite 204, Annapolis, 410-269-1132
annapolissymphony.org

# CELEBRATE THE IRISH
## IN ANNAPOLIS

With two Irish bars and an Irish gift shop downtown, Ireland is well-represented in Annapolis year-round. But things heat up every March in celebration of St. Patrick. The Hooley is a ticketed welcome party downtown, with live music, ample green lighting, and multiple bands playing traditional Irish music and Irish-tinged rock. The next two days become a much larger party called Shamrock the Dock, as bands from around the world play to diehard Irish music-loving crowds that come from all over the Mid-Atlantic.

The capper is the St. Patrick's Day Parade, which starts at Maryland Hall and makes its way up West Street, around Church Circle, then down Main Street. Throngs line up along the way to cheer on the floats and marchers, some of whom toss out swag and green beads, Mardi Gras–style.

If that's not enough Irish for you, keep an eye out for the Annapolis Irish festival, held in May and featuring a whiskey tasting tent and more live music and dancing.

naptownevents.com

abcevents.com

Annapolis Blues FC at Navy-Marine Corps Memorial Stadium

# SPORTS
# AND RECREATION

# HELP SET A RECORD
## WITH THE ANNAPOLIS BLUES

Part of the Mid-Atlantic Conference of the National Premier Soccer League, the Annapolis Blues FC played their first home game at Navy–Marine Corps Memorial Stadium in 2023. It was an immediate sensation, breaking NPSL regular season attendance records, which they broke again with a record 11,171 fans in June 2024.

How did they get a devoted fan base so quickly? The outreach started early on, with the community voting on the team's name. Season tickets are affordable and come with access to all home games, guest passes, and Blues merch. The team is heavily involved in the community, be it bringing soccer lessons to area schools or bringing kids to games. And the team itself is great, named Mid-Atlantic regular season champion in 2023 and 2024, and conference champion in 2023.

annapolisblues.com

---

### TIP

Beginning in 2025, the Annapolis Blues FC is adding a women's team, playing in the USL W League. Purchase Full Tide season tickets to get premium seats to all games, plus custom merch and perks.

# SAIL THE SEVERN
## ON SCHOONER WOODWIND

From April through October, Schooner Woodwind offers daily two-hour sailboat tours aboard twin 74-foot clipper ships that leave from Annapolis Waterfront Hotel. The purpose-built clipper ships are designed for an easy, relaxed ride, with lots of deck space. My favorite are the sunset sails, which head out at 5 p.m., bound for the Severn River and the Bay Bridge beyond. While underway, the captain points out landmarks and shares some regional history, and the crew serves up craft beer and wine when they're not working the sails. The whole thing feels like being out with friends, and it's over way too soon. They offer a frequent-sailing card, so repeat guests can earn free sails over the lifetime of the card.

80 Compromise St., Annapolis, 410-263-7837
schoonerwoodwind.com

---

## TIP

Every Wednesday, *Woodwind I* and *Woodwind II* race each other as part of the Wednesday Night sailboat races. Not only do you get an up-close view of the regatta, but you get to feel the power of a clipper pushed to her limits under the hands of an expert crew.

# REEL IN A ROCKFISH
## ON A FISHING CHARTER

Elsewhere they're called striped bass, but around here we call them rockfish, due to their penchant for hiding in rocky nooks. Noone knows them like Eastport's Captain Tom Weaver, who takes small groups out on the Bay to chase rockfish, bluefish and speckled trout. How good is he? In 2024 he set an IFGA world record for the longest striped bass ever caught and released on a fly rod.

On Kent Island, Chesapeake Bay Sport Fishing has multiple experienced captains and offers fully crewed, stocked charter boats seven days a week. While catch and release is preferred for rockfish, they can arrange fish cleaning service if you want to take your catch home.

If it's crabs you're after, Chesapeake Crabbing takes groups out in season to try their hands at trotlining. The traditional method used by commercial crabbers, it involves running a long line with bait attached at intervals, then pulling the line back aboard with hungry crabs attached.

fishwithweaver.com

chesapeakebaysportfishing.com

chesapeakecrabbing.com

# BIKE ACROSS AN ISLAND
## ON THE CROSS ISLAND TRAIL

Just across the Bay Bridge from Annapolis, Kent Island is one of the best places to explore on two wheels, due in equal parts to the flat landscape and stunning vistas. The purpose-built Cross Island Trail follows the footprint of the vanished Queen Anne's Railroad, which once ran the length of the island. Start at the easternmost point, Terrapin Nature Park, for amazing views of the Bay Bridge, then head west. The wide, paved path runs for 5.8 miles through open farmland and shady pine forest; multiple bridges along the way offer great water views in both directions. The trail ends at Ferry Point Park, where a boardwalk extends out over the marsh to a beach beyond.

Cross Island Trail
Terrapin Nature Area, Stevensville, 410-758-0835
qua.org/Facilities/Facility/Details/Cross-Island-Trail

## TIP

If you want a longer ride, turn south on Route 8 near Terrapin State Park and head for the Matapeake Fishing Pier, where you can connect with the Kent Island South Trail for an additional six miles.

# WATCH THEM CAPSIZE
## AT A LOG CANOE RACE

Log canoe sailing is a uniquely Chesapeake sport, the legacy of Native Americans who first transformed hollowed-out logs into sailing vessels. Today the boat is a single shallow hull topped with an oversized mast, intended for maximum sail size and maximum speed. Races take place all summer long, with the largest regattas held by Miles River Yacht Club, credited with reviving the sport in 1920.

The challenge with log canoe racing is that the overwhelming weight of the mast—it can be twice as high as the boat is long—and the lack of ballast make the vessels extremely tippy. To compensate, crews add long planks that extend horizontally out over the water; when underway, crews jam as many sailors as they can on the rails as moveable ballast, to counterbalance the weight of the sail. This works great until it doesn't and the boat capsizes, throwing everyone in the drink.

Miles River Yacht Club
24750 Yacht Club Rd., St. Michaels
logcanoe.com

# WALK THE WOODS
## AT ADKINS ARBORETUM

More than 600 species of native trees, grasses, and flowers grow in the 400-acre preserve, which is open year-round from dawn to dusk. Start at the visitor's center to find out what's in bloom, then head out to explore via five miles of walking paths that take you through silvery beech groves, over low marsh-spanning bridges, and across wildflower-filled meadows. Docent-led walks are offered on the first Saturday of the month. Check the online calendar for a slew of other events, covering everything from guided birding walks to drawing classes.

The reserve is self-supported via grants, donations, and their semiannual native-plant sale, with first dibs going to members. Well-behaved pooches are welcome; leashed only, please.

12610 Eveland Rd., Ridgely, 410-634-2847
adkinsarboretum.org

---

### TIP
If you want a longer hike, the arboretum connects to adjacent Tuckahoe State Park's trail system, adding another 20 miles of hiking and biking trails.

# HIKE THROUGH HISTORY
## AT GREENBURY POINT

This Navy-managed natural resources conservation area is most notable for its three 600-foot lattice towers, remnants of the original Naval Radio Transmitting Facility built between 1918 and 1938 to serve the transatlantic fleet. But that's just part of what makes it special. This land was a favored hunting ground of the Susquehanna Indians, and British colonists landed here in 1649, creating the first Colonial settlement of Anne Arundel County 46 years before the capital was moved here from St. Mary's City. Today it's a nesting site for waterfowl, including osprey, red-tailed hawks, and trumpeter swans. Tracts of milkweed provide a habitat for endangered monarch butterflies and 10 more rare, threatened, or endangered species. Hiking paths meander across the point and along the coastline, giving walkers a unique up-close look at how nature and history coexist. Check the website to see which trails are open; it's an inconsistent schedule.

410-293-9203
navymwrannapolis.com

## TIP

In 2021, the Naval Academy Golf Association attempted to raze the conservation area in order to build a second private golf course on the peninsula. Thanks to great work by Save Greenbury Point, Chesapeake Conservancy, and a host of conservation-centric nonprofits, as of press time Greenbury Point was still a preserve. Let's hope it stays that way.

facebook.com/savegreenburypoint

# DRESS YOUR GATSBY BEST
## FOR THE ANNAPOLIS CUP

Back in 1982, the Naval Academy commandant joked to a St. John's student that the Academy could beat the Johnnies at any sport. His response: "What about croquet?" Thus began the Annapolis Cup, an annual competition between the schools. Held every April, the tradition grew from a small-scale match to a roaring affair, with hordes of locals coming out dressed in their best Gatsby gear, drinking full bottles of Veuve Clicquot on St. John's front lawn, where the matches take place.

It's quieted down of late, with attendance capped, but it's still a great party, with food trucks, bar service, and live music. On game day, the Midshipmen don their classic whites while the Johnnies don whatever theme they chose; past games have ranged from Where's Waldo to full-on Viking gear. St. John's usually gets the last laugh; to date, they've won 32 of the 40 matches.

sjc.edu/annapolis/events/croquet

---

### TIP

St. John's offers much more than croquet. Keep an eye out for exhibits at the acclaimed Elizabeth Myers Mitchell Art Museum, or attend a lecture at Mellon Hall, designed by California modernist Richard Neutra.

---

# SPY ON BABY PELICANS
## ON SMITH ISLAND

Smith Island is accessible only by a 50-minute boat ride from Crisfield and is a key stop for migrating waterfowl. It's also the northernmost nesting spot for brown pelicans, who come here every spring by the thousands.

Delmarva Birding takes people out on boat tours to catch the spectacle. There's no landing allowed; boats pull up as close to shore as they can without disturbing the birds, who are much too busy to pay attention to you, focused instead on nesting and preening and swooping in and out with fresh fish for the babies. Even the seasoned captains who see this yearly get caught up in it all.

Afterward, return to Tylerton for a crab-cake lunch at Drum Point Market, then reboard the ferry for a stop in Ewell to pick up some Smith Island cake before heading home.

443-614-0261
delmarvabirding.com

---

### TIP

It's not just Smith Island. Delmarva Birding offers excursions all year long, including history-connected birding tours on the Harriet Tubman Underground Railroad Byway in Caroline County and Sunset Seabird Safaris, running from June through September out of West Ocean City Harbor.

---

# GO BACK IN TIME
## ON A SKIPJACK

The Chesapeake Bay oyster industry wouldn't have existed without the graceful skipjack. Marked by its low sides, raised bow, and single raked mast, these sailing ships were designed for maximum wind power to drag heavy dredges along the bottom of the Bay. In the late 1800s, thousands of skipjacks plied the Bay, but only an estimated 30 or so remain, mostly in private hands as work or pleasure boats. Which is why getting the chance to sail on one is such a rare treat.

Built in 1940, *Wilma Lee* had a long career as a working boat before being damaged after a run-in with the Tilghman Island Bridge. The Annapolis Maritime Museum bought her in 2018 and runs heritage sailing tours on the Severn River. In Cambridge, *Nathan of Dorchester* is an historically accurate skipjack built in 1994 that offers scheduled or private sails from Long Wharf.

| | |
|---|---|
| *Wilma Lee* | *Nathan of Dorchester* |
| 410-295-0104 | 410-228-7141 |
| amaritime.org | skipjack-nathan.org |

## TIP

If you want to see real working boats in action, helmed by the watermen who use them every day, head to Deal Island for their Skipjack Festival, held over Labor Day weekend.

Deal Island Skipjack Festival
410-784-2785, lionsclubdic.org

# PARTY WITH THE MRE
## AT THE TUG OF WAR

Eastport was its own town up until 1951, when it was annexed by the City of Annapolis. In 1998, the City of Annapolis temporarily closed the Spa Creek Bridge for repairs, to the dismay of Eastporters who had to drive the long way around to get into town. In retaliation, the Maritime Republic of Eastport formed and officially seceded. The bridge was soon reopened, but the MRE still flies its yellow flag, and the rebellion is replayed every fall at the Eastport–Annapolis Tug of War. Teams on either side strain to pull a custom 1,700-foot rope stretched across Spa Creek (or as the MRE calls it, the Gulf of Eastport), while spirited crowds chant "heave ho!" The side with the most wins gets bragging rights. It's a great excuse for a massive street party on the Eastport side, with bands, beer, food trucks, and vendors, and the revelry goes on long after the tugging ends. Proceeds go to great causes in the local community.

Eastport–Annapolis Tug of War
Second Street and Spa Creek, Eastport
themre.org/tug

# CATCH SOME SPRAY
## AT A WATER RODEO

If you think rodeos take place only on land, think again. Chesapeake Cowboys do with boats what those other ones do with livestock. Extreme docking competitions grew out of the good-natured competition between working watermen, vying to see who could dock backward at the fastest speed. Per Chesapeake Cowboys founder Erick "Flea" Emely, the first "official" rodeo took place in 1972 in Crisfield, between watermen from Smith and Tangier islands, with a dozen soft crabs as the prize. It moved between Crisfield and Deal Island for the next 20-plus years before expanding around the Bay.

People come out by the thousands to watch the competitions, often getting sprayed as the boats race at top speed for prize money. And the Chesapeake Cowboys aren't the only ones doing it. You'll find smaller locally-run water rodeos around the Bay, often done as fundraisers for the local community.

443-880-1731
facebook.com/chesapeakecowboys

# GET EYE LEVEL WITH NATURE
## AT BLACKWATER NWR

It isn't just people who find this 27,000-acre refuge so appealing; so do countless flocks of waterfowl that stop here on the annual migratory route known as the Atlantic Flyway.

Every season has its own visitors. In December and January, snow geese and tundra swans shimmer over the marshes like kinetic art installations. Spring brings migrating shorebirds and songbirds. In summer, baby ospreys and eagles test their wings, and white-tail fawns scamper in the marshland. Year-round residents include bald eagles, great horned owls, and foxes.

There are myriad ways to explore, with hiking trails and a drivable auto route that stops at different viewing platforms. But to me the best way to take it all in is by kayak, seeing the marshes at eye level. Blackwater Adventures rents watercrafts and does guided tours, searching out spots where wildfowl gather.

Blackwater National Wildlife Refuge
2145 Key Wallace Dr., Cambridge, 410-228-2677
friendsofblackwater.org

Blackwater Adventures
2524 Key Wallace Dr., Cambridge, 410-901-9255
blackwateradventuresmd.com

# CHEER ON CRUSTACEANS
## AT THE HARD CRAB DERBY

This only-in-Maryland tradition has been held every Labor Day weekend since 1947. When it began, the races took place on the street in front of the post office. These days, the hard-shelled contenders race on a track—basically a slick, fast board. The track is set up on an angle, which is more conducive to getting the crabs moving (evidently not all of them know they're racing) and easier for spectators to follow as they sidle through a series of heats until there's one crab left standing. The three-day festival also includes the Miss Crustacean beauty pageant, a crab-cooking contest, and a crab-picking contest. Live music, a 10K run, and a high-stakes boat-docking contest round out the weekend's events.

Downtown Crisfield
410-968-2500
nationalhardcrabderby.com

# PADDLE THE POCOMOKE
## IN SNOW HILL

The Eastern Shore is filled with beautiful rivers, but none are prettier than the Pocomoke, the region's easternmost tributary. This narrow, deep river passes through a Southern gothic landscape edged by the country's northernmost stands of cypress. Tannins from the trees give the river its dark appearance, and the depth (up to 45 feet) makes it brilliantly reflective. Taking to the tributary is like going back in time, with turtles nosing up for air between the lily pads and myriad types of warblers singing in the trees as you paddle the seemingly current-less water. Keep an eye out for nesting bald eagles. You may even luck out with a river otter sighting. Pocomoke River Canoe Company in Snow Hill rents canoes, kayaks, and stand-up paddleboards and offers drop-off/pick-up portage service.

2 River St., Snow Hill
410-632-3971
pocomokeriverpaddle.com

# FEAR THE GOAT
## AT A NAVY FOOTBALL GAME

The US Naval Academy brings its own traditions to game day. Of course, there's tailgating, as alumni clubs set up elaborate party tents in the parking lot of Navy–Marine Corps Memorial Stadium. The Drum & Bugle Corps marches among the gatherings, getting the crowd dancing and cheering. As kickoff approaches, the 4,400-strong Brigade of Midshipmen parades onto the field in tight formation called March On, then stands through the presentation of colors, national anthem, and a fly-over by Navy jets. During the game, any time Navy scores, a cannon is fired and the plebes rush to the end zone, doing a push-up for each point on the scoreboard. Mascot Bill the Goat (a live goat, who lives his life under strict security to prevent kidnapping by rivals) is always on hand, placidly chewing grass on the sidelines as he inspires the team to victory.

550 Taylor Ave., Annapolis
navysports.com

# RIDE THE RAILS
## IN BERLIN

It might be argued that the Eastern Shore ends at Berlin; that's where farms and fields give way to Ocean City sprawl. Berlin is charming, with great restaurants, breweries, and shops in the historic center. But to experience the landscape, board a railbike and pedal the historic railroad tracks that surround it.

Tracks and Yaks started in Frostburg, where they combine rail biking with kayaking (hence the name). But in Berlin, it's all about pedaling. Their starter trip is a six-mile round trip that goes from downtown to Ironshire Road Crossing. The longer 13-mile Queponco Excursion goes along an 1877 rail line to the Queponco Train Station, which served Belin, Snow Hill, and Newark. It closed in the 1960s and stands as a testament to how this rail line served rural communities, as well as Ocean City's burgeoning tourism scene.

12 Baker St., Berlin, 443-856-3309
tracksandyaks.com

---

### TIP
Unlike the Tracks and Yaks excursions in Western Maryland, which are primarily downhill, this is flat land. You can choose either a two-person or four-person railbike, but at least one of you will need to pedal the whole time.

---

# RUN A FOOT RACE
## OVER A BRIDGE

The Chesapeake Bay Bridge was the longest over-water steel structure in the world when it was built, stretching 4.3 miles from Sandy Point to Kent Island. This bridge is for vehicles only—except for one day in November, when runners and walkers can experience it on foot. Up to 25,000 enthusiasts register for the 6.6-mile, point-to-point race, which starts at Sandy Point State Park, heads east over the bridge, and finishes at Queen Anne's Park. Not a runner? No worries; an estimated 30 percent of participants have never done a 10K and sign up to enjoy the view from 200 feet up. If that's too daunting, sign up for the Maritime Republic of Eastport's .05K Bridge Run, held every May. This cheeky race over Spa Creek takes less than five minutes but has all the extras of a real race, including bibs, T-shirts and trophies.

thebaybridgerun.com

themre.org/bridgerun

---

### TIP

Don't feel like running? Head to the patio at Carroll's Creek Cafe for up-close views of Spa Creek Bridge, or take in the Bay Bridge from the beach at Sandy Point.

# SEE MARYLAND'S STATE SPORT
## AT REN FEST

Just outside Annapolis, the Tudor village of Revel Grove stands dormant most of the year but comes to life every fall with the Maryland Renaissance Festival. An estimated 350,000 merrymakers descend over nine weekends to enjoy actors, fire-eaters, jesters, and more at one of the nation's oldest Renaissance fairs. There is literally something for everyone: 12 stages keep up a packed slate of performances from juggling shows to Shakespeare, while strolling performers do sleight of hand or period ballads.

The biggest draw are the jousters, who face off on horseback in the packed arena. The sport originated in the Middle Ages but became popular in these parts after the Civil War and was named our state sport in 1962.

Audience participation is at the heart of Ren Fest and attendees oblige, sporting corsets, kilts, capes, and more. Don't own period duds? An onsite booth rents costumes for daily use.

1821 Crownsville Rd., Crownsville, 800-296-7304
rennfest.com

# TIP

Want more jousting? The Maryland Jousting
Tournament Association, formed in 1950,
holds tournaments all across the state.

marylandjousting.com

# SPREAD THE JOY OF SAILING
## WITH CRAB

Chesapeake Regional Accessible Boating (CRAB) has a single aim: to help anyone who wants to learn to sail, be it people with disabilities, underserved youth, or wounded warriors. The group began in 1989 when Annapolitan Don Backe suffered an accident that left him paralyzed. Friends figured out a way to get him back on his sailboat, and a movement was born.

Today, CRAB operates out of their state-of-the-art Adaptive Boating Center on Back Creek, with a floating dock and transfer equipment to get anyone from the dock into a boat. From April through October, volunteers take guests out on their fleet of 22-foot sailboats, leaving their limitations behind. There's also a power catamaran for guests who prefer not to leave their wheelchairs on the dock, and a custom Martin 16-foot sailboat with a "Sip & Puff" steering system that allows kids and adults with disabilities to sail by using their breath. Sign up to be a crew member by attending a spring training session.

7040 Bembe Beach Rd., Annapolis
crabsailing.org

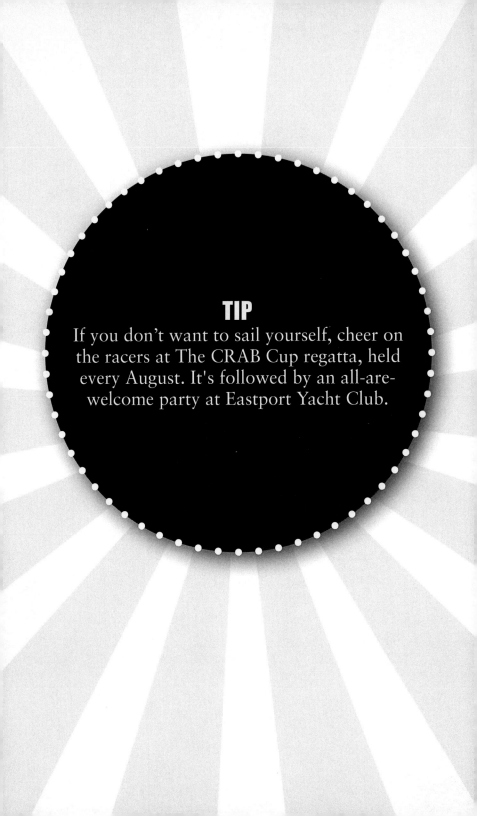

## TIP

If you don't want to sail yourself, cheer on the racers at The CRAB Cup regatta, held every August. It's followed by an all-are-welcome party at Eastport Yacht Club.

Harriet Tubman Mural, Cambridge

# CULTURE
# AND HISTORY

# DRIVE MARYLAND'S NEWEST
## ALL-AMERICAN ROAD

The designation "All-American Road" was created in 1991 by Congress to highlight our nation's less-traveled roads. To be named, the road has to have at least two nationally significant "intrinsic qualities" and be a tourism destination unto itself. There are only 60 in the US.

The original Chesapeake Country Scenic Byway ran through Queen Anne and Kent counties. A 2021 expansion earned it All-American Road status—and more federal protection. The entire route spans 419 land miles, from the C&D Canal to the Crisfield Park Pier, and another 12 nautical miles to Smith Island. It follows a general pattern along Route 213 to Route 50 and Route 413, with side spurs that extend down rural byways along the way. Instead of speeding through it, take a few days and make a true road trip out of it, stopping at small towns and overlooked historic sites along the way.

Federal Highway Administration
fhwaapps.fhwa.dot.gov/bywaysp

## TIP

In 2024, Scenic America held their first ever Byway Madness contest. The Chesapeake Country Scenic Byway came in first, besting the more famous Big Sur Coast Highway (second place) and the famed Pacific Scenic Coast Byway, which took third.

scenic.org

# WALK FOUR CENTURIES IN TWO HOURS
## WITH WATERMARK

The city of Annapolis was founded in 1649, which means there's a lot of history along these brick-paved streets and alleyways. Unlike the open-air museum that is Colonial Williamsburg, Annapolis remains a thriving city today—one that happens to have the largest intact collection of Revolutionary Era buildings in the country.

You'll get a good overview on the entertaining Colonial Annapolis Walking Tour. A guide in 18th-century garb takes you inside the State Capitol, where George Washington resigned his military commission in 1783; down narrow streets edged by 18th-century Georgian mansions and 19th-century wooden townhomes; and onto the grounds of the US Naval Academy, via the same gate Abraham Lincoln used during the Civil War. Guides put their own slant on the history, adding in anything from the life of Francis Scott Key to the tale of the doomed craftsman said to haunt the State House dome.

410-268-7601
watermarkjourney.com

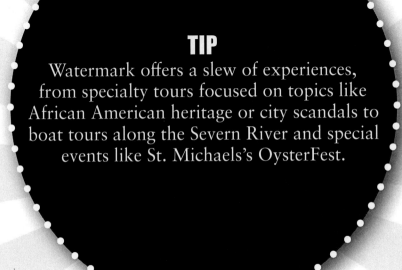

**TIP**
Watermark offers a slew of experiences, from specialty tours focused on topics like African American heritage or city scandals to boat tours along the Severn River and special events like St. Michaels's OysterFest.

# MARK THE MASON–DIXON LINE
## IN MARDELA SPRINGS

Back in 1763, Charles Mason and Jeremiah Dixon were hired to help settle a long-running dispute between the Calvert and Penn families over conflicting land charters between the Colonial states of Maryland, Pennsylvania, and Delaware. They traveled the country for the next four years, measuring and marking the border with stones. Most of the stones have been lost to time and development, but one of the southernmost markers still stands near Mardela Springs. Located on an unassuming roadside pullout off rural Highway 54, an iron-gated gazebo protects the centuries-old relic from hands or theft. There are actually three stones here: two smaller stones placed by field scouts and an unrelated stone thought to have been moved here by a well-meaning farmer. The star is the 3.5-foot-high crownstone made of English limestone and engraved on opposite sides with the Calvert and Penn coats of arms, verified by Mason and Dixon themselves in 1764.

Trans-Peninsular Line Midpoint Marker
Rt. 54 near Mardela Springs
visitmaryland.org

# DISCOVER THE FLEET
## AT CHESAPEAKE BAY MARITIME MUSEUM

This 18-acre waterfront complex showcases Chesapeake maritime life past and present. Exhibits range from a warehouse replicating the oyster industry to an explorable circa-1879 lighthouse moved here from Hoopers Strait.

Their floating fleet is the largest collection of Chesapeake boats in the world and includes the 1889 *Edna E. Lockwood*, the oldest sailing bugeye still afloat. Some boats are available for tours. A tour on the double-decker steamboat *PATRIOT* teaches about the town's history, area ecology, and secrets of the mansions only visible from water's edge. Or book a private boat and head out for up-close views of the log canoe races run from Miles River Yacht Club. At press time, restoration on their beloved 1920s oyster boat *Winnie Estelle* was almost complete, so she will be able to rejoin the fleet for tours.

213 N Talbot St., St. Michaels, 410-745-2916
cbmm.org

---

### TIP
To see how it all works, visit their working shipyard and watch current restoration projects, done by full-time staff shipwrights as well as apprentices via their Shipwright Apprentice program.

# SEE WHERE DEMOCRACY WON
## AT THE MARYLAND STATE HOUSE

Established in 1772 (though not finished until 1797, due to the Revolutionary War), the Maryland State House is the oldest state house in continuous legislative use. A statue of George Washington in the Old Senate Chamber marks the exact spot where he resigned as commander in chief of the Continental Army in 1783, ceding his own personal power to ensure that the United States remain a democracy following the Revolutionary War.

The House remains the seat of government for the Maryland General Assembly, and you can see the assembly rooms when it's not in session. Other must-sees include a Charles Willson Peale painting of Washington, Lafayette, and Tilghman; portraits of Maryland's four signers of the Declaration of Independence; and a copy of Washington's resignation speech displayed under glass. The domed roof, which is the highest point in Annapolis, is the largest wooden dome constructed without nails, capped off with a lightning rod designed by Benjamin Franklin.

100 State Cir., Annapolis, 410-974-3400
statehouse.maryland.gov

**TIP**

The State House is open to visitors every day of the year except Christmas and New Year's Day. Self-guided tour information is available onsite. Photo IDs are required for entrance, as is a metal detector scan.

# SAIL A TALL SHIP
## AT DOWNRIGGING WEEKEND

In fall 2001, schooner *Sultana* and clipper ship *Pride of Baltimore II* took a sail down the Chester River, marking the end of the season before taking down their rigging for the winter. The crews had so much fun that they decided to repeat the voyage the next year. It has since grown into the *Sultana* Downrigging Festival. Every fall in Chestertown, *Sultana* and *Pride* are joined by other tall ships—including *Maryland Dove*, a reconstruction of one of the ships that landed near St. Mary's County in 1634—in the largest annual gathering of tall ships in North America. Sign up for a public sail to experience them on the water and attend lectures to learn more about their place in maritime history.

In the last few years, organizers have upped the fun by adding a bluegrass festival, with three days of music to go alongside a food-truck gathering, children's village, and Friday night fireworks show on the waterfront.

Downtown Chestertown, 410-778-5954
downrigging.org

---

### TIP

Both ships operate as educational ships and make their rounds of the Bay and points further afield, inviting visitors aboard at port calls. Get the schedules at sultanaeducation.org and pride2.org.

---

# TIME TRAVEL
## AT HISTORIC LONDON TOWN

Located on the South River, London Town was established in 1683 as a ferry stop on the route from Annapolis to parts north; consider it the Route 50 of its day. Unlike the Revolutionary-era millionaire mansions you'll find in Annapolis, this open-air museum reflects its history as a working-class port town that would have been populated by carpenters, ironsmiths, and traders. The centerpiece is the stately William Brown House, built as a tavern in the 1700s. You'll also find a recreated wood-plank tenement house and a woodworking studio, both built to Colonial-era design. Costumed reenactors bring the place to life, be it at monthly events like Colonial Cocktails or events like Revolutionary London Town, showcasing life in 1776.

839 Londontown Rd., Edgewater, 410-222-1919
historiclondontown.org

---

## TIP

Nature lovers will enjoy the eight acres of trail-laced woodland gardens. A loyal band of volunteer gardeners keep it beautiful, whatever the season.

# FOLLOW THE UNDERGROUND RAILROAD
## ON THE HARRIET TUBMAN BYWAY

Freedom fighter Harriet Tubman was born enslaved in 1822 in Dorchester Country, and escaped bondage in 1849 with a harrowing run north to Philadelphia. Despite facing possible capture and death, she returned to Maryland at least 13 times to rescue other enslaved people from the extensive network of plantations on the antebellum Eastern Shore. Start off at the US Park Service's Harriet Tubman Underground Railroad National Historic Park, where multimedia exhibits shed light on her daring escape and return visits to free family and friends, along with a greater context of the realities of life in that era. Then get in your car and head out on the Harriet Tubman Byway, which winds for 125 miles through the countryside. There are 36 stopping points along the way, including Brodess Farm, where she was born; the still-intact Bucktown General Store, where Tubman was seriously injured in an altercation involving an enslaved person and an enraged overseer; and Choptank Landing, near where she made her first escape.

Harriet Tubman Underground Railroad National Historic Park
4068 Golden Hill Rd., Church Creek, 410-221-2290
nps.gov/hatu

**TIP**

In Cambridge, stop at the Harriet
Tubman Museum & Educational Center
to see the moving mural by Michael
Rosato depicting a determined
Tubman reaching a hand out to
those who need her help.

424 Race St., Cambridge
harriettubmanmural.com

# MEET AN ENGINEERING MARVEL
## AT THE C&D CANAL

In the 1600s, Dutch settler Augustine Hermann had an idea: Dig a canal connecting the Delaware River to the Chesapeake Bay to cut short the 300-mile ocean trip between Philadelphia and Baltimore. Work finally began in 1824, and after five years of hand digging, the Chesapeake and Delaware (C&D) Canal opened. A series of locks helped boats through the 14-mile passage until the 1970s, when dredging made them unnecessary. Today, the active shipping channel is a picturesque way-through for ships, edged by Chesapeake City's quaint blocks of Victorian-era homes turned into shops, restaurants, and B&Bs.

Start your visit at the museum, where the original steam-powered lifting wheel is on display in the stone pumphouse. Then stroll along the water's edge via the Ben Cardin C&D Canal Trail, gazing in awe at the towering tankers and cruise ships that pass through what is still one of the busiest canals in the world.

85 Bethel Rd., Chesapeake City, 410-885-5622
chesapeakecity.com

# SEE THE SHIP MODELS
## AT THE NAVAL ACADEMY MUSEUM

Located in Preble Hall, the US Naval Academy Museum is often overlooked for the more scenic parts of the Academy. But it's a treasure trove, spanning the history of the Navy from the Revolutionary War to the present, highlighting alumni participation in everything from space exploration to Nobel Prizes. Most intriguing to me is the display of 17th- and 18th-century ship models, representing almost every type of war ship from the 1600s rendered in exquisite detail. It's considered one of the best collections in the world, and contains ship models made by French POWs from the bones of their beef rations during the Napoleonic Wars.

After you've toured the museum, head to the nearby US Naval Academy Chapel and pay your respects to the Navy's founding father at the Crypt of John Paul Jones, located in a room beneath the main chapel.

118 Maryland Ave., Annapolis, 410-293-2108
usna.edu/museum

# RIDE THE NATION'S
## OLDEST PRIVATE FERRY IN OXFORD

The channel separating the towns of Oxford and Bellevue is less than a mile wide, but if you can't go across it, you need to drive 30 miles around the headwater of the Tred Avon River to get to the other side. Enter the Oxford–Bellevue ferry, which began operation in 1683 and remains the oldest privately owned ferry route in the country. Walk or drive onboard at the Oxford landing and 10 or so minutes later, you'll dock in even tinier Bellevue. You can disembark or take the ride back to Oxford; the boat runs on a continuous circuit every 15 to 20 minutes. Vintage photo displays share the history of the ferry, and the journey is always fun, especially if you're lucky enough to catch the last ferry of the day, just before sunset, when the golden light reflects off the water and the ospreys are returning home after their last fishing trips of the day.

101 E Strand Ave., Oxford, 410-745-9023
oxfordferry.com

---

### TIP
Like the best things in life, this one is limited, with service running daily from mid-April through October, and weekends only in November. At press time it was for sale.

---

# EXPLORE AN URBAN WATERWAY
## ON SPA AND BACK CREEKS

The Eastport Peninsula is bordered by two very different waterways: Spa Creek and Back Creek. Spa Creek flows past historic City Dock, the flanking outposts of Annapolis Yacht Club, and million-dollar marinas and homes. Quieter Back Creek, once the province of hard-working watermen, is home to the majority of working marinas in the city.

There's no better way to experience them than by boat. And you have loads of options on how to do it. Annapolis Canoe and Kayak rents kayaks, canoes, and stand-up paddleboards from their marina-side shop in Eastport, all of which are for sale if you like the fit. Don't feel like paddling? Annapolis Electric Boat Rentals offers 10-seat electric boats for hourly rentals, no boating experience needed. Or leave the driving to someone else with a water taxi ride or a 40-minute guided tour of Spa Creek aboard Watermark's *Miss Anne*.

Annapolis Canoe and Kayak
311 Third St., Suite B, 410-263-2303
annapoliscanoeandkayak.com

Annapolis Electric Boat Rentals
300 Second St., 443-433-2129
aebrentals.com

Watermark
1 Dock St., 410-268-7601
watermarkjourney.com

# BURN YOUR SOCKS
## FOR THE EQUINOX

Back in the 1970s, an Eastport resident decided to welcome the vernal equinox (and unofficial start of boating season) by burning the socks he'd worn all winter. He invited a few friends to join him, and thus a uniquely Annapolis tradition was born. The biggest event takes place at the Annapolis Maritime Museum, where a who's who of locals and prominent politicians come to say goodbye to winter, burning their socks on a giant bonfire at an afternoon party featuring live music, shucking contests, and all-you-can-eat oysters. If you don't want to fight the crowds (or can't get a ticket—it's always a sellout), look for the more casual sock burning held by the Maritime Republic of Eastport, or set up your own around a fire pit. After all, traditions are meant to be shared.

723 Second St., Annapolis, 410-295-0104
amaritime.org

# ODE TO THE EQUINOX

by Jefferson Holland, Poet Laureate of Eastport, 1994

Them Eastport boys got an odd tradition
When the sun swings to its Equinoxical position,
They build a little fire down along the docks,
They doff their winter shoes and they burn their
    winter socks.

Yes, they burn their socks at the Equinox;
You might think that's peculiar, but I think it's not.
See, they're the same socks they put on last fall,
And they never took 'em off to wash 'em, not at all. . .

So they burn their socks on the Equinox
In a little ol' fire burning nice and hot.
Some think incineration is the only solution,
'Cause washin' 'em contributes to the
    Chesapeake's pollution.

Through the spring and the summer and into the fall,
They go around not wearin' any socks at all,
Just stinky bare feet stuck in old deck shoes,
Whether out on the water or sippin' on a brew.

So if you sail into the Harbor on the 20th of March
And you smell a smell like Limburger sautéed with
    laundry starch,
You'll know you're downwind of the Eastport docks
Where they're burning their socks for the Equinox.

# CLIMB INSIDE
## THOMAS POINT LIGHTHOUSE

An icon of the region, Thomas Point Shoal Lighthouse has been guarding the mouth of the South River since 1875 and is the only screw-pile lighthouse on the Bay still in its original location. It's beautiful from the water, but even cooler inside. Sign up for a tour done in conjunction with the US Lighthouse Society. The 30-minute boat ride takes you from Eastport to the lighthouse, giving great photo ops as you approach. Once docked, docents take you up a steel ladder and inside the structure for an hour-long tour, detailing everything from an 18th-century lightkeeper's tasks and lifestyle to its current work as an active Coast Guard beacon. On your way out, say hi to Drew, the coyote decoy that stands sentry on the dock. His job is to look lifelike enough to keep birds (and bird guano) away from the lighthouse, and he's great at it.

thomaspointshoallighthouse.org/tours

---

### TIP

Tours are offered most weekends from June through early October and are capped at 18 people. They sell out, so book early.

---

# JOIN THE REBELLION
## AT THE CHESTERTOWN TEA PARTY

The Boston Tea Party gets all the ink in the history books, but it wasn't the only protest of its kind. Back in 1774, when the citizens of Chestertown learned that the British had closed the port of Boston, they responded by passing a resolution that banned the import, sale, or consumption of tea and tossed their own chests of tea into the Chesapeake.

OK, so some historians dispute that last part, but Chestertown celebrates the story each year with a weekend-long party held Memorial Day weekend. There's a tea-tossing reenactment and a Colonial-style parade. But the highlight is the raft race, where competitors create their own floating designs from non-nautical materials for a race on the Chester. (Spoiler alert: Not all of them float.) Street vendors, a heritage village, food trucks, and mobile bars round out the fun.

Downtown Chestertown, 410-778-1361
chestertownteaparty.org

# HONOR THE MIDDLE PASSAGE
## AT CITY DOCK

Alex Haley's epic novel *Roots* became a worldwide phenomenon, telling the story of Haley's ancestors, who were brutally kidnapped and enslaved. Annapolis is one of the documented Middle Passage locations where enslaved people—including Haley's great-great-great-grandfather Kunte Kinte—were auctioned off, and it's designated by UNESCO as a Site of Memory of the Slave Route Project.

The history is detailed in the commemorative plaque, and memorials around City Dock add to the story. Life-size bronze statues depict Haley reading to children—a reminder that history needs to be taught, not hidden—and adjacent plaques share different passages from the book. A granite-and-bronze compass dial shows a map of the world with Annapolis at its center. Together with a depiction of ship conditions and a slave auction listing from a 1767 issue of the *Maryland Gazette*, the memorial provides a powerful reminder of this horrifying era of American history and serves as a testament to the power of the human spirit.

City Dock, Annapolis

**TIP**

Every September, the city comes alive with music, dancing, and spoken word at the Kunte Kinte Heritage Festival, which celebrates 35 years in 2025.

240-801-5543
kuntakinte.org

# DIG INTO SMALL-TOWN ROOTS
## IN DENTON

Rural museums can be time machines, showcasing the past through treasured memorabilia from the community. In landlocked Caroline County, the history is rooted in agriculture. This homespun museum opens in an 1819 home and runs through a series of connected buildings. Much of what is on display is donated from the local community. A reconstructed circa-1824 log cabin with period furnishings shows how people lived in the county's early days. A map follows the Underground Railroad through Caroline County, and the WWII exhibit displays photos, newspaper clippings, and belongings of locals who went off to fight in the war, many of them not making it home. The museum also works to save local buildings from destruction; to date, they've preserved 48 structures.

16 N Second St., Denton, 410-479-2055
carolinehistory.org/rural-life-museum

---

### TIP

Every county has historical societies and museums that preserve the stories of generations past. Get the list via Maryland State Archives at msa.maryland.gov.

---

# WELCOME MAY DAY
## IN DOWNTOWN ANNAPOLIS

Back in 1955, the Garden Club of Old Annapolis Towne invited residents and businesses in the downtown historic district to put out baskets for May Day. It's grown into an annual tradition, drawing onlookers to downtown Annapolis to enjoy the bounty of creativity.

Participants are asked to put a floral display in a basket or container on their doors or stoops by 10 a.m. on May 1, when members of the Garden Club of Old Annapolis Towne begin walking around for the judging, awarding blue ribbons to favorites. The winners are invited to a private tea held two days later in a historic home.

You'll see everything from small door bouquets on private residences to creative shop-themed displays and overflowing floral installations outside restaurants that become Instagram sensations. Locals come out in droves to stroll the streets, snapping pics and chatting about their favorites as they celebrate the onset of spring.

downtownannapolispartnership.org/may-day-baskets

# SEE THE BLUE ANGELS
## FROM THE WATER

One of the best things about living in Annapolis is getting multiple chances to see the Blue Angels. The team of six F/A-18 Hornets performs every year on the Wednesday before USNA commencement, thrilling viewers with their daredevil rolls, loops, and precise formations above the Severn River. There's no better way to get a sense of how low and fast they can go than by seeing them from the water, which is why thousands of boaters get there early to drop anchor with the best vantage points.

Don't have access to a boat? Watermark offers sightseeing cruises aboard the *Harbor Queen* and *Lady Sarah*, and Capital SUP organizes a group trek of kayaks and stand up paddleboards.

If you can't get out on the water, get as close to it as possible. Great viewing spots include Ingram Field and Hospital Point on the Naval Academy campus; Jonas Green Park under the Severn River Bridge; and Spa Creek Bridge in Annapolis.

blueangels.navy.mil

Watermark Cruises
410-268-7601
watermarkjourney.com

Capital SUP
410-919-9402
capitalsup.com

# TIP

The Blue Angels always do a practice session the day before the big show, broken into morning and afternoon. It's a great way to see them with fewer crowds. On Commencement Day, they do a low pass over Navy–Marine Corps Memorial Stadium as a salute to the graduation class.

# ENJOY A DICKENS CHRISTMAS
## IN CHESTERTOWN

With the publication of *A Christmas Carol* in 1843, Charles Dickens put his forever stamp on the holiday season with his tale of the redemption of Ebenezer Scrooge. Chestertown takes that book as the inspiration for their annual Dickens of a Christmas festival, held in early December. The historic downtown filled with Victorian-era buildings makes the perfect backdrop for the two-day celebration.

Horse-drawn carriages clop down cobblestone streets, and storefronts are adorned with strings of greenery and twinkling lights. The town square transforms into a vibrant marketplace, with vendor stalls selling gifts, bites, and warm drinks. Costumed carolers break into song, roving jugglers wow onlookers, and the main stage plays host to music from bagpipes to chamber orchestras. Locals dress up in period duds, and there's a Victorian costume rental shop at the Welcome Center. It's a celebration that would make Scrooge himself happy.

mainstreetchestertown.org/dickens-festival

# WATCH THE SUN SET
## IN ROCK HALL

There isn't a lot to do in Rock Hall, and that's the point. It's faster to get here by boat from Annapolis than it is to drive, which explains why there are more marina slips than hotel rooms. Whether you stay onboard or on land, your activities are pretty much the same. Stroll the cute downtown shops (some only open on weekends) and join the locals at Ferry Park beach. Wander out for wildlife viewing at Eastern Neck National Wildlife Refuge, less than 10 miles from town. Dig into fresh seafood at one of the family-owned restaurants, or catch live music at happy hour. When it comes time for the sun to make her descent, head back to Ferry Park (or anywhere on Beach Road) to watch the nightly show. Rock Hall faces west overlooking the Bay, so the sunset views are unbeatable.

rockhallmd.com

---

### TIP

Rock Hall gets raucous every August, when costumed revelers take over the street for the annual Pirates and Wenches Weekend. Enjoy sea-shanty singalongs, plentiful rum tastings, street vendors and live music at this three-day party.

rockhallpirates.com

# MEET FOUNDING BLACK FAMILIES
## AT WATER'S EDGE MUSEUM

Our home would not be what it is without the survival skills and sacrifices of our earliest residents, many of them brought here enslaved to work the plantations around the Eastern Shore. Opened in 2021, Water's Edge Museum tells the story of the area's founding Black families—some of whom can trace their lineage back to pre-Revolutionary War days—through art, literature, and photography.

The museum grew from the discovery of a series of paintings by Rose Starr Ross in the 1930s that capture the lives of Black families in Talbot County in the early part of the 20th century. The discovery led descendants of the paintings' subjects to share their own family heritage, via stories and keepsakes, and the museum was born. The curators use mixed media from drawings and photographs to literature, paired with more details via QR codes, to tell the stories of sailmakers and farmers to towns like Unionville, our nation's only town founded by formerly enslaved Civil War soldiers.

101 Mill St., Oxford, 410-226-1227
watersedgemuseum.org

# PERUSE THE GALLERIES
## OF EASTON

Art lovers will find plenty of inspiration in the cultural hub of the Eastern Shore. The acclaimed Troika Gallery represents a curated group of artists working in oils, pastels, watercolors, and bronze. The Academy Art Museum features a permanent collection with works from Ansel Adams, Mary Cassatt, and Francisco Goya, among others, and brings in juried artists for curated shows and their annual Craft Show. Zach Gallery is the newest on the scene, showcasing contemporary artists from around the world in their gallery at the Prager Family Center for the Arts.

Troika Gallery
troikagallery.com

Academy Art Museum,
academyartmusuem.org

Zach Gallery
zachgalleryeaston.com

---

## TIP

Every November, throngs of visitors take in the best in nature-inspired artwork at the three-day Waterfowl Arts Festival, which also boasts live bands, a tasting pavilion dedicated to MD-made goods, and the competition for best goose- or duck-caller at the World Waterfowl Calling Championships.

waterfowlfestival.org

# GET THE FULL STORY
## WITH HISTORIC ANNAPOLIS

For two centuries of an expanding Annapolis, developers tore down old buildings with no thought. In the early 1950s, a few local women took umbrage, organizing to move the Carrol House to St. John's College for safekeeping, and later purchasing the circa-1715 Shiplap House to protect it. In the 1960s, they fought to keep the USNA from expanding past Gate 3 and then went on to purchase and restore historical homes, from the grand William Paca House to humble, wood-frame Hogshead.

But Annapolis isn't just about buildings. At the Museum of Historic Annapolis, chronological exhibits over multiple floors tell a rich tale of the city's people, from the early days when the Sons of Liberty met under a tree on the St. John's campus, plotting revolution, to the Civil Rights era, when community leaders marched arm-in-arm to prevent riots in the wake of Martin Luther King's death.

99 Main St., Annapolis, 410-990-4754
museum.annapolis.org

## TIP

Another project of Historic Annapolis is their historic marker program. Pick up or download the guide, then walk around town looking for the octagonal markers on private homes. They're color-coded, depending on era and architectural style, covering 1715 to 1938.

# FOLLOW THE LIFE
## OF FREDERICK DOUGLASS

Abolitionist leader Frederick Douglass was born enslaved in Talbot County before escaping at age 20 and heading north, where he became the most prominent orator and author of his day. Opened in 2018 on the 200th anniversary of his birth, Frederick Douglass Park on the Tuckahoe seeks to capture the landscape of his childhood, which he so vividly recalled in his books. A life-size sculpture at Talbot County Courthouse in Easton marks where he gave his groundbreaking "Self-Made Men" speech to a segregated audience in 1878. He built his retirement home in the African American summer community of Highland Beach, outside Annapolis; though he never actually lived there, it's now a small museum, open by appointment. Learn more about him and the greater context of African American culture at the small but robust Banneker–Douglass–Tubman Museum, located in an 1874 brick church in downtown Annapolis.

# DISCOVER MORE ABOUT FREDERICK DOUGLASS

Frederick Douglass Park on the Tuckahoe
13211 Lewiston Rd., Queen Anne, 410-770-8050
frederickdouglasspark.org

Frederick Douglass Museum and Cultural Center
3200 Wayman Ave., Annapolis
fdmcc.org

Banneker–Douglass–Tubman Museum
84 Franklin St., Annapolis, 410-216-6180
bdmuseum.maryland.gov

# MEET THE WATERMEN
## OF TILGHMAN ISLAND

The bascule bridge spanning Knapps Narrows has a clearance of just nine and a half feet and is manned by bridge tenders 24 hours per day, 365 days per year. The busiest drawbridge on the East Coast (and one of the busiest in the world), it opens an estimated 12,000 times per year for boaters taking a shortcut between the Choptank and the Bay.

Most of the traffic is commercial watermen. A block away, the Tilghman Watermen's Museum spotlights this heritage. Striking paintings give a glimpse of what the island was like when the Tilghman Packing House employed more than 600 workers. A video shows men working the boats, and exhibits detail pound nets, trotlines, and oyster tonging. But what makes this museum so special is that docents have a personal connection to the exhibits, and watermen pop by in their downtime to share stories.

6031 Tilghman Island Rd., Tilghman Island, 410-886-1025
tilghmanmuseum.com

## TIP

The museum is in one of Tilghman's signature W houses. Built between 1890 and 1900, this architecture style is unique to the island. Of the 13 original structures, only two remain standing in their original form today.

# STROLL THE CAMPUSES
## OF USNA AND ST. JOHN'S

St. John's College was founded in 1696 as King William's School and focuses on a Great Books liberal arts curriculum. The USNA was founded in 1847 to educate future Navy and Marine Corps officers. Vastly different in style and size, the two are just blocks apart and easy to tour in one long walk.

Start at USNA, entering through Gate 1 by the Visitor's Center. (Note: USNA is an active military base, so ID is required and access may be restricted at times.) Enjoy the Severn River views from the sea wall, then admire the historic houses on Captains Row and the copper dome of the USNA chapel. End up in front of Bancroft Hall, where the entire brigade lines up daily in precise rows for noon meal formation.

Exit via Gate 3 and walk the two blocks to St. John's, which spans a mere 36 acres. The main lawn leads up to circa-1742 McDowell Hall, the oldest building on campus. Pop into the Mitchell Art Museum, and end your walk at Hodson Boathouse, overlooking College Creek.

United States Naval Academy
usna.edu

St. John's College
sjc.edu

# CELEBRATE THE SEASON
## AT A LIGHTS PARADE

Every December, a one-night-only transformation takes over Annapolis Harbor. As the winter sky darkens, boats gather silently in Spa Creek, lining up to make their debut. At precisely six o'clock, the signal sounds, and all the boats press the on button, transforming the scene into a brilliant spectacle of seasonal lights. For the next two hours, the costumed boats parade in and out of Ego Alley, lights flashing and carols blasting, while spectators lined up along City Dock and Spa Creek Bridge marvel at their creativity. And what creativity there is, from tugboats dressed up as Rudolph to a boat transformed into the wood-paneled station wagon from *National Lampoon's Christmas Vacation*. A panel of judges chooses the official winners, with prize money going to each. But this is really a case where just showing up is reward enough; it's a highlight of the holiday season.

Eastport Yacht Club
844-INFO-EYC
eastportyc.org/lights-parade

### TIP

Can't make it to Annapolis? Most waterfront towns around the shore do their own smaller-scale parades, including Chesapeake City, Rock Hall and St. Michaels.

Maryland Avenue

# SHOPPING
# AND FASHION

# DISCOVER AN ARTISAN
## AT LOCAL BY DESIGN

Susan Sears had a great idea: Curate a collective of local makers and give them a place to shine. What started at a warehouse in the Annapolis Arts District has turned into a three-gallery showplace for local artisans, from artists in traditional mediums like watercolors to furniture makers, jewelry designers, and craftspeople.

Their flagship gallery on the corner of Maryland Avenue has rotating pieces from over 100 artists; a larger collection awaits at their gallery at the Annapolis Mall. And their original location in the Annapolis Design District still thrives, with 30 artisans set up in a warehouse. Once a month, they do an evening Market at the Gallery, where artists, vendors, and shoppers mingle over cocktails.

Downtown
41 Maryland Ave., 443-833-3925

At the Mall
1705 Annapolis Mall, 443-951-8221

At the Gallery
1818 Margaret Ave., 410-268-2500

localbydesignannapolis.com

## TIP

Want something custom? She'll connect you with the artist directly. To learn how to create something yourself, check out their hands-on workshops in practices such as glass work and jewelry making.

# BUY A BOAT
# (OR PRETEND TO)
## AT THE ANNAPOLIS BOAT SHOWS

Thinking about buying a boat? Then head to the largest in-water boat show in the country, which takes over downtown Annapolis for two weekends in October. One week is devoted to sailboats, the other to powerboats. Even if you're not in the market for a vessel, it's fun to take in the spectacle. Dealers from around the country showcase their latest models along miles of purpose-built floating docks, and most let you explore with climb-aboard tours. If you're new to cruising, onsite instructors will take you out on the Severn River and teach you the basics. And the boat show isn't just about boats; it's about the boating lifestyle, with vendors showcasing everything from the latest in galley kitchenware to nautical-themed art and snazzy duds that would look great on your imaginary yacht.

410-268-8828
annapolisboatshows.com

## TIP

Can't make it for the fall boat shows? Visit in April for the Spring Sailboat Show, held in Annapolis, and the powerboat-focused Bay Bridge Boat Show, on Kent Island.

# FALL IN LOVE
## WITH MARYLAND AVENUE

In the 1800s, this two-block stretch was *the* shopping street for downtown residents. It still is for me. The 1873 opera house facade is still visible, as is the Art Deco theater marquee above Ka-Chunk!!, an indie record store. Every great street needs a great bookstore, and they have that in Old Fox Books & Coffeehouse. For clothing and accessories, try Cupla, owned by twin sisters. There are three local art galleries, including fine art at Jo Fleming. For gifts, snacks, or a bottle of wine, head to Annebeth's. Like antique stores? Maryland Avenue has four of them. (Evergreen is my favorite.) And every great street needs a great pub, which you'll find at Galway Bay. The view looking up the brick-lined street to the State House is pure magic in every season.

The Maryland Avenue Fall Festival, held every October, is one of the longest-running fairs in the state and always on my calendar. As you roam the blocks from shop to shop, enjoy live music, vendors galore, and a slew of costume-clad critters in the Halloween Pet Parade.

Maryland Avenue & State Circle Business Association
mascma.com

# EAT CIDER DONUTS
## AT HOMESTEAD GARDENS

This garden/decor/whatever-else-you-need store is the largest enclosed garden center in Maryland, drawing landscapers and gardeners from around the region. And it's great year-round, with more than 333,000 square feet of growing space tending to annuals, perennials, trees, and shrubs in every color and variety you can imagine, plus all the supplies you need to keep them happy and healthy. Not a gardener? You'll also find chic outdoor furniture, a huge assortment of grills, women's apparel and accessories, even something for Fido or Mittens. (Bring Fido along; the whole place is dog-friendly.)

But, to me, it's best in the fall, when their mammoth Fall Festival brings hayrides, live bands, a petting zoo, and a beer garden every weekend in September and October. Plus, it's the only time of year you can get their made-to-order cider donuts.

743 W Central Ave., Davidsonville, 410-798-5000
homesteadgardens.com

# RUN OUT THE CLOCK
## AT MIDNIGHT MADNESS

The first three Thursday evenings in December, downtown shops in Annapolis stay open late so people can do their holiday shopping. But it's not just about shopping; the historic area turns into a cold-weather street party. Performers set up on street corners, playing holiday favorites, and carolers stroll in and out of shops, singing harmonies. Many shops offer libations, from cider to champagne, so people can sip as they shop, and bars and restaurants overflow as people meet up with friends over the course of the night. You never know what you'll run into: a llama petting zoo in Main Street, hot cocoa and bonfires in the courtyards of shops along Maryland Avenue, shoppers taking selfies in Snowflake Alley, or the Naptown Brass Band starting a seasonal second line with the Grinch on City Dock.

December Thursdays from 6 p.m. till late
downtownannapolispartnership.org/midnight-madness

---

### TIP
The Downtown Annapolis Partnership is a nonprofit 501c(3) aimed at getting people out and about with events from the carving of giant pumpkins at Halloween to Annapolis Restaurant Week in late February. They're a great resource for events and specials.

· · · · · · · · · · · · · · · · · · · · · ·

# INVEST IN AN HEIRLOOM
## AT RECLAIMED

The tagline here is "Rebuilding History One Piece at a Time," and that's exactly what they do. Owners Mark and Tracy Miller's passion is reclaiming antique wood and materials and restoring or repurposing them into heirloom-quality pieces. This isn't a thrift-store, chalk-paint makeover. They source from a wide network around the country, and do research on the provenance of every piece, with the aim of creating impeccable quality family heirlooms with a proven link to the past.

Originally in St. Michaels but relocated to downtown Annapolis, Reclaimed focuses on furniture, while their sister shop, the Boathouse, has a maritime-meets-mid-century bent. That said, you never know what you'll find in each, be it a curio chest made from old-growth wood, a pristine set of vintage glassware, or an impeccably restored neon sign. That's part of the fun.

129 Main St., Annapolis
36 Market Space, Annapolis, 267-221-5107
reclaimwoodworks.com

# SUPPORT POSITIVITY
## AT HALF FULL GIFT BOUTIQUE

We all need more positivity these days. And that's the point behind this shop on Kent Island. Owners Laurie Mastroberti and Stacie McGinnis wanted to create a place that spread joy and made a difference for customers and the greater world. The well-curated shop has something for everyone, from housewares to art to jewelry, and the team goes out of their way to make visiting a joyful experience, offering warm welcomes and help selecting that perfect something. They focus on supporting vendors that make a difference, be it via local artisans and craftsmen, fair-trade practices, or seeking out companies that give a portion of proceeds to their communities. The result: a shopping experience that makes you feel better about the world and helps make the world a better place.

480 Main St., Suite 100, Stevensville, 443-249-3008
halffullshop.com

# BAG THE PERFECT BAG
## AT HOBO

I'm always on the lookout for the perfect bag: equal parts chic and useful, with the right number of pockets, and well made enough to take a beating. Which is why I'm such a fan of HOBO. Their bags are sold in shops across the country, but their only standalone store is a three-story townhouse at the foot of Main Street. The bright, loft-style space sells a wide array of backpacks, totes, purses, and wallets. Their smart designs include practical details like easily accessible cell-phone pockets hidden in seams and cool accents from grommets to fringe that reference the boho 1970s without being trendy or overdone. If you're on a budget, head up to the second floor, where they keep their sale items. That's where I typically get into the most trouble.

194 Green St., Annapolis, 410-349-5081
hobobags.com

# FILL YOUR NEEDS
## AT PEMBERTON PHARMACY & GIFT

Back in the early part of the 20th century, the neighborhood drug store was a go-to for prescriptions and medical care but also sundries, gifts, and quick groceries. You used to find them all over the country, but a very few still exist in today's world of corporate chain stores. That's what makes this one so special.

Family-owned Pemberton Pharmacy & Gift is a true working pharmacy, with a large counter and pharmacist on hand. While you wait for your prescription, wander the rest of the store, finding everything from clothing to books to makeup to toys to groceries. It's a testament to the town's support that they are still thriving, both as a local go-to and a popular pop-in for visitors.

204 S Talbot St., St Michaels, 410-745-8382
pembertonpharmacy.com

# CONNECT OVER WORDS
## AT OLD FOX BOOKS & COFFEEHOUSE

A great indie bookstore has a welcoming staff, a well-curated selection of books, and a varied slate of events that build community. Old Fox Books & Coffeehouse has all that and more, in a cozy setting pairing historic brick walls with cushy armchairs, patterned rugs, a fireplace, and a communal table ideal for book club meetups. Upstairs are newer books, notecards and journals, and an outpost of Brown Mustache Coffee. A spiral staircase leads to a stone-walled basement holding a treasure trove of used books organized by subject. A suit of armor stands sentry on the back deck, where wooden steps lead down to their best-kept secret: the beautiful back garden, decorated with café tables and strands of Edison lights. It's the kind of place where fairy tales aren't just sold, but they happen.

35 Maryland Ave., Annapolis, 410-626-2020
oldfoxbooks.com

---

### TIP
Want more bibliophile friends? Join one of their book clubs (they typically run two to three) or an event like an author reading, story time with Frolic the Fox or Pirate Joe, or whatever else they dream up that month.

---

# MORE COOL INDIE BOOKSTORES

## Book Hounds

Opened in May 2024, this bookstore is a delight for the eyes, from whimsical decor and nooks for storytime to a beautifully curated selection of reads. It's exactly the kind of bookstore St. Michaels has been waiting for.

104 N Talbot St., St. Michaels, 410-745-8070
bookhoundsmd.com

## The Bookplate

You could easily get lost among the stack-filled rooms at this Chestertown favorite, which specializes in gently worn used books plus select new and regional titles. It's a must for me whenever I'm in town.

112 S Cross St., Chestertown, 410-778-4167
facebook.com/bookplatebookstore

## Vintage Books and Fine Art; Flying Cloud Booksellers

These shops are a block apart but entirely distinct. Flying Cloud has a beautiful selection of new books, from fiction to design, food and art, and a lovely kids' section. Vintage focuses on rare and used books, and works directly with collectors.

4 N Washington St., Easton, 410-562-3403
vintagebooksmd.com

26 W Dover St., Easton, 410-775-5311
flyingcloudbooks.com

# CAPTURE THE BAY
## WITH JAY FLEMING

Photographer Jay Fleming comes by his career naturally. His father was a photographer for *National Geographic*, and when Jay was given his father's hand-me-down Nikon at age 13, he followed suit. In the decades since, he has devoted his life to capturing the beauty and traditions of Chesapeake Bay. He's the author of two acclaimed books, *Working the Water*—about watermen and their traditions—and *Island Life*, focusing on Smith and Tangier islands. You'll also find his work at Annapolis Collection Gallery, alongside other celebrated photographers like Aubrey Bodine and Charles E. Emery. Keep an eye out for Jay's annual holiday party and show, held every December. He's always on hand to discuss and sell his work, or sign copies of his books.

jayflemingphotography.com

Annapolis Collection Gallery
55 West St., Annapolis, 410-280-1414
annapoliscollection.com

## TIP

Jay leads hands-on photography workshops, taking small groups out on the water. Join a day class in Annapolis or a weekend trip farther away, from Smith Island to Maine. Contact him at jaypfleming@gmail.com for more info.

# FIND THE PERFECT GIFT
## AT TWIGS AND TEACUPS

Opened in 1991 by sisters April and Eugenia Marshall, Twigs is the area go-to for gifts, picks-me-ups, and things you didn't know you wanted until you saw them there. When the sisters retired in 2014, the community held its breath until the Heckles family bought it, promising to keep the same vibe.

Extensive renovations on the circa-1922 building opened the second floor to expose the original wooden rafters, added modern amenities like an elevator, and more than doubled the retail space, meaning twice the finds. Downstairs are kitchenwares, books, curios, and more; upstairs are clothing, shoes, accessories, and more gifts. Last time I was there, I went in vowing to buy nothing and came out with French milled soap, a cribbage board, and gifts for two friends. That's Twigs.

111 S Cross St., Chestertown, 410-778-1708
facebook.com/twigsteacups

# ACTIVITIES
## BY SEASON

## WINTER

Run Out the Clock at Midnight Madness, 125

Enjoy a Dickens Christmas in Chestertown, 106

Celebrate the Season at a Lights Parade, 117

Enjoy the Masters with the Annapolis Symphony, 50

Get a Jolt at Rise Up Coffee Roasters, 6

Slam an Oyster Shooter at Middleton's, 2

Hum Along with the USNA Glee Club, 38

Get Classical at St. Anne's, 46

## SPRING

Bike Across an Island on the Cross Island Trail, 57

Spy on Baby Pelicans on Smith Island, 63

Dress Your Gatsby Best for the Annapolis Cup, 62

Reel in a Rockfish on a Fishing Charter, 56

Honor the Middle Passage at City Dock, 100

Celebrate the Irish in Annapolis, 51

Welcome May Day in Downtown Annapolis, 103

See the Blue Angels from the Water, 104

Join the Rebellion at the Chestertown Tea Party, 99

Burn Your Socks for the Equinox, 96

# SUMMER

# FALL

# SUGGESTED
## ITINERARIES

## FOR THE LOVE OF BOATS

Sail a Tall Ship at Downrigging Weekend, 88

Climb Inside Thomas Point Lighthouse, 98

Meet the Watermen of Tilghman Island, 114

Explore an Urban Waterway on Spa and Back Creeks, 95

See the Ship Models at the Naval Academy Museum, 93

Go Back in Time on a Skipjack, 64

Spread the Joy of Sailing with CRAB, 76

Sail the Severn on Schooner Woodwind, 55

Buy a Boat (or Pretend to) at the Annapolis Boat Shows, 122

## WHERE TO GET OUTDOORS

Paddle the Pocomoke in Snow Hill, 70

Reel in a Rockfish on a Fishing Charter, 56

Explore an Urban Waterway on Spa and Back Creeks, 95

Spy on Baby Pelicans on Smith Island, 63

Hike through History at Greenbury Point, 60

Bike Across an Island on the Cross Island Trail, 57

Walk the Woods at Adkins Arboretum, 59

Ride the Rails in Berlin, 72

Get Eye Level with Nature at Blackwater NWR, 68

Spend the Weekend at a Music Festival, 48

• • • • • • • • • • • • • • • • • • • • • •

## GREAT EXCUSES FOR A ROAD TRIP

## FUN FOR FAMILIES

## ONLY IN ANNAPOLIS

• • • • • • • • • • • • • • • • • • • • • • • • • •

## QUINTESSENTIAL EASTERN SHORE

# INDEX